good dog behaviour
AN OWNER'S GUIDE

Gwen Bailey

Gwen Bailey is a well known Animal Behaviourist and a past Chairman of the Association of Pet Behaviour Counsellors. She has a B.Sc. (Hons) degree in zoology and has worked for The Blue Cross since 1988 when she became the first person to be appointed by a national UK animal welfare charity as a full-time animal behaviourist. Gwen has been successfully solving behaviour problems in dogs rehomed by The Blue Cross. She also advises owners who are thinking of giving up their dogs, thereby helping them to get rid of the problem rather than the dog.

Gwen gives lectures at numerous national and international conferences, runs training courses for staff at other animal charities, has written many educational leaflets and is also the author of the *Collins Puppy Handbook*.

AUTHOR'S ACKNOWLEDGEMENTS

I would like to thank John Rogerson, my friend and mentor, who has taught me so much about dogs. This book has been possible because of my association with him and I am grateful to him for sharing his knowledge with me so that I too, could help dogs and their owners.

I would also like to thank five treasured and talented friends whose comments on the first draft of this book improved it immeasurably. They are Julie Sellors, Stephen Sanders, Tony Orchard, Joanne Hetherington and Andrew Edney. Their support during the tedious days of writing was also much appreciated.

Finally, I would like to thank The Blue Cross who have employed me as their Animal Behaviourist for more years than I first thought possible. My work with them has allowed me to help so many dogs and their owners and to clear up the misunderstandings that existed between them. It is my hope that through the pages of this book, I will be able to help prevent similar misunderstandings from happening in the future.

For Winnie the Ridgeback, a loyal friend and
part of my life for the past 11 years.

good dog behaviour
AN OWNER'S GUIDE

GWEN BAILEY

First published in hardback in 1998 by HarperCollins*Publishers*, London

First published in paperback in 2002 by Collins
An imprint of
HarperCollins*Publishers*, 77-85 Fulham Palace Road, Hammersmith, London W6 8JB

The Collins website address is www.collins.co.uk

07 06 05 04 03 02
9 8 7 6 5 4 3 2 1

A catalogue record of this book is available from the British Library

ISBN 0 00 714256 0

This book was created by SP Creative Design for HarperCollins*Publishers* Ltd
EDITOR: Heather Thomas
DESIGN AND PRODUCTION: Rolando Ugolini
All photography by David Dalton except the following:
Gwen Bailey: pages 66, 102 and 126; Rolando Ugolini: pages 1, 7, 9, 12, 13 (top right), 14 (bottom), 15 (top), 17, 18, 19, 25, 26, 27 (bottom), 31, 35 (top), 52, 58, 61, 62, 87, 97 (top), 100, 101, 103, 121, 123 and 125.

The publishers would like to thank the following for their kind assistance in producing the book: Scampers School for Dogs, Northfield Road, Soham, Nr. Ely, Cambs. for their help with providing dogs for photography; The Blue Cross, Shilton Road, Burford, Oxfordshire and their staff for providing dogs and facilities for photography; Ginny Mabbot and Jacky, Joanne Hetherington and Prince, Claire Millington and Zaa Zaa, Selina Williams and Henry, Nile Mason and Fanny, Samantha Visick and Oscar, and Nicola Parkinson. The publishers would also like to thank; Philip and Cherie Sutton and Ben, Luan and Carole Brame and Simba, Tony Martin and Misty, Joanna and Zena Ugolini and Sam, David Marland and Skimble, and Thirza and Max Rockall and their dogs Milo and Gunner.

Colour reproduction by Colourscan, Singapore
Printed and bound by Printing Express Ltd, Hong Kong

Note: Throughout this book, 'he' rather than 'he/she' or 'it' has been used. This is to make the text easier to read and does not reflect on the relative worth of male or female animals. Dogs of both sexes make good pets, and both sexes have their own disadvantages and positive attributes.

CONTENTS

FOREWORD

By The Blue Cross

Dogs are a part of our daily life and they mean many things to many people. They are a source of inspiration to artists, writers and sculptors; they feature in films and television programmes; and their images are used to sell a whole range of products. Dogs were once kept mainly as working animals, but, in recent times, their principal role has changed to one of being a companion to share our lives. For a dog to be good company, it must be contented and have all its needs met. Only then can it behave in a way that allows us to enjoy living with it in our homes. Without a job to do, a companion dog must be given an outlet for its energies and some purpose in life. It will then be free to act in a way that we, as owners, can approve.

Sadly, all too often, relationships between pets and their owners break down due to a lack of understanding or appreciation of dogs' special needs. The resulting bad behaviour forces owners to try various methods of punishment to no avail. If those relationships cannot be mended in time, the greatest loser is the dog who loses its home and is rejected by the people it knows and loves. If it is lucky, it will find itself in rescue kennels, like those of The Blue Cross. There it may languish for some time before a new owner can be found who is willing to take on the dog and its problems. In addition, the original owners who raised the dog lose a much-loved pet and may, worse still, without recognising their mistakes, go on to raise another puppy with the same bad habits.

The Blue Cross's commitment to animal behaviour work stems from the belief that if owners understand their pets better, fewer dogs will 'go wrong' and be given up or abandoned. Owners who have developed a greater understanding of dog behaviour, make better owners who are kinder to their animals. Thus, the lives of the animals they own may improve considerably.

This book attempts to achieve a greater understanding between dogs and their owners and is fully supported by The Blue Cross. All relationships need to be worked at to be successful and the alliance between dog and owner is no exception. With the help of this book, you can achieve an understanding with your dog which will go beyond words, and the result will be a well behaved dog with whom you can look forward to spending many more happy years.

CHAPTER ONE

ALL DOGS CAN BE WELL BEHAVED

Almost every owner would like a dog that is loyal, friendly, never naughty and obeys their every command. Most people, however, live with a dog whose behaviour is less than perfect and are tolerant of a wide variety of behaviour that does not conform to their idea of good conduct. However, it is possible for everyone to have a well-behaved dog. All that is required is that the owner develops a better understanding of their dog and

BELOW: *Terriers enjoy games with toys that squeak because they were bred to catch and kill small animals.*

changes the way they behave towards him. This book will help you to do this.

WHY IS YOUR DOG LIKE HE IS?

A dog's adult character depends on both the genes passed on to him by his parents and ancestors and the environment he has lived in throughout his life. Both will have an effect on his personality, his temperament and qualities, and, consequently, on the way he behaves.

Genetic influences in dogs are very profound. Our present-day dogs are all descendants of the wolves. Wolves are efficient predators of large prey that hunt

co-operatively in packs. To do this they need to be sociable and communicative; both traits that make them excellent precursors of our domestic dogs.

In addition, the wolves have an instinctive hunting behaviour which gave them a suitable template to exploit in order to produce the working breeds. We selected the qualities we most admired and created a whole range of dogs to suit different purposes. Different breeds have specific traits that their ancestors required for their 'job'. For example, Collies are born with a strong instinct to chase and herd moving objects, Terriers enjoy shake and kill games, particularly with objects

Below: Puppies learn about each other's strengths and weaknesses as they play together.

that squeak, Dachshunds and Terriers which are bred to 'go to ground' like to dig, and Bull Terriers like to hang on to objects and tug.

While genes have given our dogs the blueprint for behaviour, the environment in which they live helps develop and strengthen behaviour patterns. Dogs that are raised and kept in different situations will have different characters. Thus, for example, a pet dog raised from a very early age in a kind home with lots of children and animals is likely to be friendly, playful and sociable, whereas a dog kept shut away for most of the time is

ABOVE: *A Springer Spaniel is likely to be energetic and enjoy retrieving because of his genetic make-up.*

likely to be shy and fearful. A dog raised with overbearing owners will possibly have a low opinion of his own abilities whereas a dog kept with very indulgent, easy-going owners is likely to be more confident.

Experiences early in life, particularly during the first year, will have the most influence on future character. However, dogs are very adaptable and will continue to change their behaviour as a result of experiences and influences from their surroundings throughout their lives.

It is impossible to say whether genes

THE CANINE HUNTING SEQUENCE

The hunting sequence of the wolf is as follows:

1	TRACK AND FIND PREY
2	FIX GAZE ON PREY AND FREEZE
3	STALK
4	CHASE
5	GRAB BITE
6	KILLING BITE
7	DISSECT
8	CONSUME
9	RETRIEVE AND BURY WHAT HE CANNOT CONSUME

Man has accentuated different parts of the hunting sequence to create dogs that are suitable for various types of 'work'.

2 & 9: Gundogs
2, 3 & 4: Herding breeds
1 & 4: Hounds
5 & 6: Terriers

or environmental factors have more influence on the dog's adult character. Both play their part and are inextricably linked. Both should be considered when trying to understand why a dog is like he is.

WHICH BREED IS RIGHT FOR YOU?

Acareful choice of a puppy or an adult dog will ensure that you acquire a dog with a genetic make-up that suits you.

1 LABRADOR RETRIEVER
◆ **BRED FOR** retrieving fish and game from icy water

◆ **ACTIVITY LEVEL:** ◆◆◆
◆ **CHARACTERISTICS:** good-tempered, very agile, biddable

BELOW: *Labradors are natural swimmers and enjoy retrieving objects from the water for their owner.*

LEFT: *German Shepherd dogs can be territorial and are often protective.*

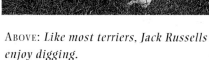

ABOVE: *Like most terriers, Jack Russells enjoy digging.*

4 JACK RUSSELL TERRIER
- ◆ **BRED FOR** killing rats and foxes
- ◆ **ACTIVITY LEVEL:** ◆◆◆◆
- ◆ **CHARACTERISTICS:** alert, courageous, tenacious

5 WEST HIGHLAND WHITE TERRIER
- ◆ **BRED FOR** killing rats and foxes
- ◆ **ACTIVITY LEVEL:** ◆◆◆◆
- ◆ **CHARACTERISTICS:** active, resolute, high self-esteem

2 GERMAN SHEPHERD DOG
- ◆ **BRED FOR** herding and guarding
- ◆ **ACTIVITY LEVEL:** ◆◆◆◆
- ◆ **CHARACTERISTICS:** alert, attentive, tireless

3 BORDER COLLIE/ WORKING SHEEP DOG
- ◆ **BRED FOR** herding sheep
- ◆ **ACTIVITY LEVEL:** ◆◆◆◆◆
- ◆ **CHARACTERISTICS:** persistent, hard-working, compliant

LEFT: *West Highland White Terriers will shake and 'kill' toys.*

6 GOLDEN RETRIEVER
◆ BRED FOR
retrieving game
◆ ACTIVITY LEVEL: ◆◆
◆ CHARACTERISTICS:
alert, attentive, tireless

LEFT: *Golden Retrievers*

7 ENGLISH SPRINGER SPANIEL
◆ BRED FOR flushing and
retrieving game
◆ ACTIVITY LEVEL: ◆◆◆◆◆
◆ CHARACTERISTICS: friendly, biddable,
energetic

BELOW: *Springers' boundless energy, agility and willingness to please make them ideal working dogs.*

ABOVE: *A Cocker Spaniel in full flight flushing out game.*
RIGHT: *Staffordshire Bull Terriers are courageous and fearless.*

8 COCKER SPANIEL
- ◆ **BRED FOR** flushing and retrieving game
- ◆ **ACTIVITY LEVEL:** ◆◆◆◆
- ◆ **CHARACTERISTICS:** bustling, exuberant, affectionate

9 STAFFORDSHIRE BULL TERRIER
- ◆ **BRED FOR** fighting other dogs
- ◆ **ACTIVITY LEVEL:** ◆◆◆
- ◆ **CHARACTERISTICS:** courageous, tenacious, fearless

10 YORKSHIRE TERRIER
- ◆ **BRED FOR** killing rats
- ◆ **ACTIVITY LEVEL:** ◆◆◆
- ◆ **CHARACTERISTICS:** alert, intelligent, spirited

BELOW: *Yorkshire Terriers are spirited little dogs which enjoy playing.*

ABOVE: *Boxers are affectionate, exuberant and boisterous. They can make lovely pets providing they get enough play and exercise.*

11 CAVALIER KING CHARLES SPANIEL
- ◆ **BRED FOR** companionship
- ◆ **ACTIVITY LEVEL:** ◆
- ◆ **CHARACTERISTICS:** affectionate, friendly

12 BOXER
- ◆ **BRED FOR** hunting bears and boars
- ◆ **ACTIVITY LEVEL:** ◆◆◆◆
- ◆ **CHARACTERISTICS:** lively, strong, loyal

MONGRELS AND CROSS-BREEDS

Mongrels contain elements of their various 'pure bred' parents. They will have a real mixture of genetic traits which can be accentuated or played down by their owners as they are raised. They are good 'all-round' dogs and often make excellent pets.

Cross-breeds (from pure-bred parents of different breeds) contain a mixture of the characteristics of both breeds. They have the advantage over pure-breeds of having fewer health problems associated with inbreeding. The most successful crosses are often those where a breed with a gentle, placid nature is crossed with a breed with a more reactive temperament.

THE RIGHT DOG FOR THE RIGHT SITUATION

When looking at the characteristics for each breed, you should realise that there is a negative side to each quality if it is incorrectly channelled. For example, it may be beneficial to have an 'alert' dog that responds to all your requests quickly, but a dog that is alert and responsive to every little noise

BELOW: *Exercise requirements are not always dependent on size. The giant Irish Wolfhound, for example, is often less active than other smaller dogs.*

outside would become very tiresome.
Similarly, it may be nice to have a
'lively' and 'energetic' dog if you have
a high activity level yourself, but on
days when you have no desire to be
very active, this energy may emerge in
unwanted activity and bad behaviour.

ABOVE: *Any surplus energy in active*
dogs can be channelled into energetic
games with toys.

Choosing the characteristics that best
suit your requirements is essential to
achieving a happy partnership.

YOU CAN TEACH AN OLD DOG NEW TRICKS!

The old saying that 'You can't teach an old dog new tricks' is simply not true! One of the requirements of a hunting/scavenging existence is that you need to be adaptable. This trait has been handed down to our domestic dogs and they remain flexible in their behaviour and open to change throughout their lives. Unacceptable dog behaviour can be channelled into more acceptable avenues and new patterns of behaviour can be developed. With a better understanding, many owners can have dogs that are well behaved and can change their dog's behaviour for the better.

Although it is relatively easy to change the way in which a dog behaves, it is unlikely that you will be able to change a dog's character fundamentally once he is mature. A shy, submissive dog, for example, is unlikely to become a super-confident extrovert. Being realistic about how much you can change the way your dog behaves is important, but, with knowledge, understanding and some effort, even the most unruly of dogs can be tamed.

Older dogs may take more time to learn new ways because you will be working against established behaviour patterns. However, all dogs will readily pick up new ways of behaving if it is to their advantage to do so.

THE PERFECT PUPPY

If you take on a puppy, you start with a relatively clean slate. Raising a puppy takes a lot of time and effort but at least the mistakes, or lack of them, will be all yours.

Most ways of achieving good dog behaviour are common to both adult dogs and puppies and are covered elsewhere in this book. However, a most important area that relates specifically to puppies is that of socialization. One of the primary requirements of a pet dog is that he is friendly with people and other animals.

BELOW: *It is unwise to buy a puppy that is older than eight weeks unless he has been well socialized with humans.*

This will depend on the quantity and quality of social contact he gets with them as he grows up.

The early weeks of a puppy's life are very important, particularly up to the age of twelve weeks. During this time, a puppy will approach anything unfamiliar without caution. Meeting plenty of people, including children, as well as other animals, makes it more likely that he will be unafraid and sociable with them in later life.

As a puppy gets older, he becomes more apprehensive of the unfamiliar and,

VACCINATIONS VERSUS SOCIALIZATION

You will also need to protect your puppy from contagious diseases until such time as he has developed sufficient immunity against them. Consult your veterinary surgeon for information on the disease conditions in your area and how to keep your puppy safe. There is always a balance to be found between keeping your puppy protected from disease and preventing him from growing up shy and unfriendly because of a lack of social contact. With care, it is possible to reach a compromise and keep your puppy healthy while ensuring that he socializes enough to become confident and friendly towards people and other dogs.

as a result, socialization becomes more difficult. For this reason, it is essential that a puppy is obtained from a source

RIGHT: *Take particular care if your puppy is shy or sensitive, and give him more opportunities to overcome his fears.*

where every care has been taken to ensure that the socialization process is well underway before he reaches you. Never be tempted to buy a puppy from someone who will deliver him or who has numerous litters of puppies, often from different breeds, for sale. Only buy from a place where puppies are kept in a home environment or where each puppy has been given enough individual attention to make him confident and outgoing.

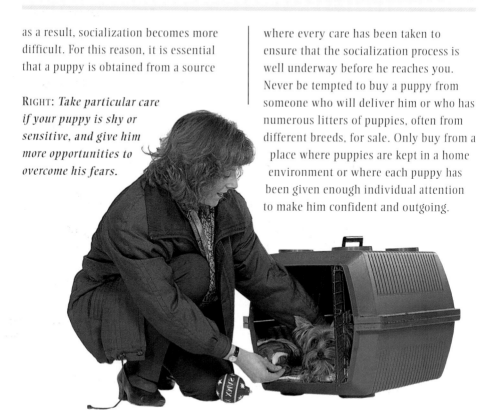

It is also unwise to buy a puppy that is older than eight weeks unless he has been kept separately from other dogs and has learned to relate well to people. Obtaining a puppy that has spent a long time playing with other dogs rather than people can result in a dog that is less than ideal as a pet.

Once you have collected your puppy, you will need to continue the important socialization process that has been started (or make up for lost time if it has not). Take your puppy out and about as much as possible, meeting a wide variety of people of different ages and characters. Take care not to overwhelm your puppy with too much at first and allow him to make all the approaches. Socialization

will need to be continued until your puppy has become a mature adult to ensure that he remains friendly and interested in people throughout his life.

Take particular care if your puppy is shy or sensitive, and allow him more time to come out of his shell. Make sure that every experience he has with people and other animals is pleasant. Watch his body language (see page 33) to determine whether or not he is enjoying the experience and take action if he is not. Try to think ahead and prevent him from having any unpleasant experiences. If all of his early life is happy and enjoyable, he will grow up with a view of the world as a safe, comfortable place. This will allow him to be friendly and outgoing.

RIGHT: *Having plenty of happy times with children and adults helps a puppy grow up into a friendly adult.*

CHAPTER TWO

SPEAKING YOUR DOG'S LANGUAGE

The reason why dogs make such popular pets is that they are so like us in many ways. However, their similarities to us can often deceive us into thinking that they are just like us in all ways; that they are a less complicated, furry version of ourselves or our children. We often expect them to think and act like small people. They cannot. All they can be are dogs. What is frequently overlooked is that they are members of a completely different species and, as such, often have surprising differences which can be the cause of problems between us. Understanding what dogs can and cannot do, and knowing their physical and mental limitations, is essential to having realistic expectations about their abilities.

THEIR PHYSICAL WORLD

It may seem too obvious to say that dogs experience things at a different level to us. But imagine what it must be like to live in a world where you cannot see the faces of the animals you live with when they walk around and where most of the interesting things they do, such as eating, take place way above your head. What must it be like to live in a house where you cannot see out of the windows without making a special effort and where most of the focus of your world is at knee height? Getting down to their level and looking at things from their perspective gives a surprisingly different view of the world we both inhabit.

RIGHT: *Dogs need to adapt their behaviour when living in a world designed for humans.*

A DOG'S SENSES

PAWS AND JAWS

Again, it may seem obvious, but dogs have no opposable thumb. This means that they cannot pick up objects easily with their paws and, instead, will often use their mouths in situations where we would use our hands. Dogs do not hit people when upset but bite instead. They can learn to be very accurate with their mouths and, once experienced, will only rarely make unintentional contact with their teeth on human skin. In other words, if a dog snaps, but misses, he probably meant to! Dogs will also explore using their mouths in the same way as we

BELOW: *The need to explore new objects with their mouths can often get dogs into trouble.*

A SMELLY FACT

A weak solution of salt is odourless to humans but dogs are able to detect as little as one teaspoonful in thirteen gallons of water.

will touch unusual objects. Since their mouths are full of teeth that can cause damage, this exploratory behaviour often gets them into trouble, particularly when they are puppies.

Another striking difference between our species is that, as primates, we like to touch, hold, hug and cuddle to express affection. However, dogs rarely do this to each other unless they are fighting or mating. This accounts for why some dogs will bite when hugged or stroked, especially by children. In order for dogs to accept our loving behaviour, they need to become accustomed to it gradually, preferably during puppyhood.

SUPER SCENTING

One of the first things a dog will do in a new environment is to put his nose to the floor and sniff. A human in the same situation would look around. A dog when meeting another dog or a person will, characteristically, sniff them, sometimes in the most embarrassing, but smelliest, places. A human (fortunately!) will just look. Both are gathering information about their world, but the way in which they do it illustrates one of the most important differences between them. We live in a very visual world, whereas dogs live in a very smelly one.

Their sense of smell is incredible by our standards. Not only do they have many more cells in their nose for detecting different smells (the area used for smell detection is fourteen times the size of ours), but these cells are of better quality and the part of their brain that

ABOVE: *Smells on the ground need careful investigation.*

receives the information is considerably more developed. This allows dogs to detect and identify a much wider variety of scents at much lower concentrations.

Using this ability enables them to acquire much more information in one

BELOW: *Dogs gather a lot of information by sniffing at places in a territory which have been marked by other dogs.*

SCENT CAMOUFLAGE

Rolling in substances with a very strong scent has never been fully explained. It is likely that it is a remnant of the days when dogs' ancestors needed to camouflage their own scent to be more like that of their environment in order to be more successful when out hunting.

sniff than we can ever imagine. Going for a walk and sniffing the scents left behind by other dogs must be like watching a video of all those who have passed by in the past few days. Information such as sex, health and social standing may be passed on through urine and faeces. This allows most male dogs, and some females, to advertise their presence and status by marking every available lamp-post and clump of grass.

Although we cannot even begin to understand what it is like to be able to detect odours in the same way as our dogs do, knowing that they live in a different sensory world can help us to understand them better. It helps to explain some of their peculiar habits, such as sniffing everything they come into contact with, kicking up earth with their back hind legs after going to the toilet (they have scent glands in between their pads), and rolling in substances that we would rather they did not.

SENSITIVE SIGHT

Dogs can see less well than humans. They can see colours but not as well as we can, and they cannot differentiate easily between certain colours, such as red and green. A dog looking for a red ball, for

EMPLOYING A DOG'S SUPERIOR SENSES

Man has utilized the dog's incredible sense of smell in a variety of ways. To detect drugs, explosives, to find lost people, to track criminals, to find buried survivors after earthquakes or avalanches, to track animals to be hunted, or, more recently, to sniff out dry rot and termites in buildings, to find human bodies lost in water or to detect skin cancers and other diseases. In such exercises, dogs are better than any machine, having a better publicity value, being more accurate, more reliable, cheaper, and more fun!

SEEING THINGS DIFFERENTLY

Dogs have a greater field of vision than humans. This enables them to see things to the rear and sides. The amount of overlap (shaded area) will determine how well the animal can judge distances.

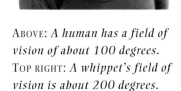

ABOVE: *A human has a field of vision of about 100 degrees.*
TOP RIGHT: *A whippet's field of vision is about 200 degrees.*

RIGHT: *Dogs that have been bred to look more like us, such as the King Charles Spaniel, with forward-facing eyes, have a reduced field of vision.*

RIGHT: *Long-coated breeds with hair that hangs over their eyes will have their field of vision greatly reduced. It is best to clip it or tie it back so that they can see properly.*

example, on green grass is more likely to be using his nose than his eyes.

They do, however, see better than us when less light is available. A reflective layer at the back of their eyes allows them to make better use of the light entering the eyes by trapping and reusing it. This is why their eyes shine eerily when they are caught in car headlights or a torch beam.

While we are able to make out static shapes easily and can quickly differentiate between two objects, dogs see things better as soon as they move. They can detect movement on a very small scale, helping them to be efficient hunters. In our world, it enables them to notice subtle body movements, which allow them to detect, a fraction of a second before we have said anything, that we are about to take them for a walk.

IMPRESSIVE HEARING

Dogs can hear better than we can. Firstly, they hear sounds more acutely. For example, a sound that can just be heard by a person 100 metres away, can be heard by a dog for up to 450 metres. Secondly, dogs can hear sounds of a higher frequency. Our range is up to about 20 kHz whereas

OPPOSITE: *Dogs with long, fluffy ears, such as Cocker Spaniels, are likely to be less good at sound detection and location.*

SOUND SENSITIVITY

Dogs that were once used for herding, such as Collies, have very sensitive hearing and, as a result, are more likely to find it difficult to live in very noisy environments and are more prone than other dogs to developing noise phobias.

dogs can hear sounds up to at least 35 kHz, allowing them to hear in the ultrasonic range. They also seem to be able to discriminate between two sounds that appear the same to us. It is probably this sense more than any other that has led people to believe that dogs have a 'sixth' sense. Because of their superior hearing, for example, dogs may become aware of the arrival of their owner long before a person sitting in the same room. A dog can hear things that we cannot, such as a 'silent' dog whistle, and may alert us to the presence of intruders or other noises in the environment long before we have heard anything.

MOVABLE EARS

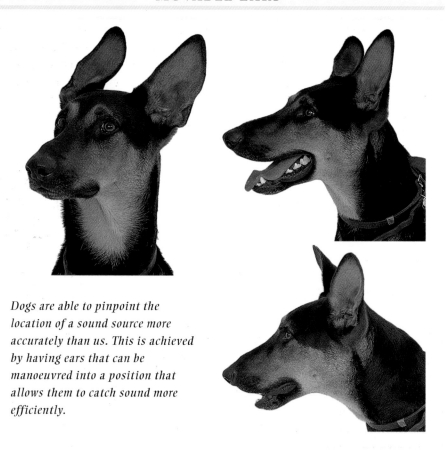

Dogs are able to pinpoint the location of a sound source more accurately than us. This is achieved by having ears that can be manoeuvred into a position that allows them to catch sound more efficiently.

DIFFERENT METHODS OF COMMUNICATION

Everyday communication between adult dogs relies mostly on body posture and scent exchange with very little in the way of vocalization. In comparison, we rely very heavily on the spoken (or written) word and only use body signals and scent in very subtle and secondary ways.

BODY LANGUAGE V. SPOKEN WORD

Knowing no better, dogs will assume that our methods of communication are similar to their own and will attempt to communicate using body postures and signals. Owners need to know what to look for so that they do not miss these vital signs from their pets.

In addition, dogs will also watch our body language to try to find out what we want them to do. This is why dogs learn hand/arm signals so much more quickly than they learn spoken commands. Pointing out the direction you want your dog to take, using an obvious arm and hand movement, is surprisingly effective, and especially so once he has become familiar with the signal. If your dog, for example, has just brought a recently unearthed bone in from the garden and is about to drop it on the carpet, shouting at him to go out may not be effective. Asking him to go out, leading the way and pointing out the direction you intend him to take with a clear hand and arm movement, will give him a much more obvious message about the action you require him to take.

PLAYBOW
The universal invitation to play. A sudden drop into this position usually results in a frantic bout of tag between two playful dogs. If directed at a human, the dog is asking if you would like to play a game.

RIGHT: *The playbow is an obvious invitation to play.*

FEARFUL DOG

Frightened dogs will have a lot of their weight on their back legs ready to run. Their head is held high ready for a defensive bite if necessary. They hold their tail low or tucked in, ears drawn back but not pinned flat against the head. They will often pant in short, sharp breaths and may yawn a lot. In extreme cases, or if the dog is afraid for too long, they may begin to shake or tremble. The whites of their eyes can be seen as their eyes are held as wide open as possible. The pupils are often wide open and consequently the eyes may have a reddish tinge to them. If the eyes appear red and glassy, the dog is very fearful and should be approached with caution as he may well bite in self defence. The hair along the back of the neck (the hackles) and along the spine may also be raised, especially if he is

BELOW: *This dog's tail is lowered and his ears are drawn back in a fearful posture.*

fearful of other dogs. These make a dog look larger than he really is and help to reduce the chances of him being attacked.

Dogs that are anxious but not yet very fearful will exhibit some or all of these signs in varying degrees. Watching for subtle clues that your dog is ill-at-ease can help you to take the appropriate action sooner rather than later and may help to prevent your dog from becoming scared or aggressive.

ABOVE: *A happy greeting from your dog involves vigorous wagging of his tail and rear end.*

HAPPY DOG

A dog that is pleased to see you will wag his tail, sometimes the rear half of his body as well, press his ears back to the sides of his head and pull the corners of his mouth back in greeting.

Happy dogs appear relaxed and their bodies will be soft and not tense. They will eat readily and will be happy to play games and be handled. A pet dog should be relaxed, calm and happy most of the time.

CONFIÐENT DOG

A confident dog will hold his head and tail up and his body erect, proudly displaying his strength and purpose. He will often have

RIGHT: *This confident dog has an erect posture with head and tail held high.*

a 'presence' which encourages you to pay attention to him and will appear to be very self assured.

Very confident dogs rarely use aggression to get their own way since they are sure of their ability to do so without

using force. Less confident dogs, however, are less sure of their abilities and may resort to confrontation if they think they will lose. Confident dogs will have had many successful encounters with other individuals during their lifetime and are often very good at communicating with others.

SUBMISSIVE DOG

A submissive dog will make himself as small as possible to deter attack from a

ABOVE: *Adopting a submissive position helps to turn off aggression and signals an intent to appease.*

ANGRY DOG

An angry dog will often become very still and stiff just before he bites. This period of stillness gives him time to weigh up the opposition and gives the opponent a chance to back down or submit. If you find yourself in a situation where you have done something to make a dog react in this way, for example, you have stroked a dog that did not want to be touched, be very careful what you do next. Keep very still and retreat very slowly.

Signs to look for:

◆ Stillness and a rigid posture.

◆ Eyes fixed and staring.

◆ Conflicting signals of confidence and fear, for example, tail held high, head high, eyes wide and pupils dilated, hackles raised.

When a dog becomes angry, adrenalin flows around the body and other changes occur that help to sustain any action that may be taken. For this reason, it is best to isolate an angry dog and let him calm down for at least half an hour before approaching him again. If your dog has had a bad experience, he is likely to be more reactive for a few days after the incident so care should be taken until he has recovered.

stronger member of the pack. By showing appeasing gestures, such as lip licking, he is more likely to be tolerated by the stronger individual.

SUBMISSIVE GRIN

This greeting looks ferocious but is, actually, totally harmless. The submissive grin is seen more often in specific breeds, such as the Dalmatian, and seems to be their way of greeting important individuals. They will also grin in this way when told off, giving rise to the theory that it is some form of appeasement gesture.

TAIL WAGGING

A wagging tail is not, necessarily, an indication of friendly intent. It is, however, a sign of an excited, aroused state. Happy dogs will wag their tails in a sweeping side-to-side motion. Frightened dogs will often hold them low with just the tip wagging. A confident dog about to bite will often hold his tail high and stiffly wagging.

ABOVE: *A young Jack Russell puppy approaches slowly. It is cautious and reserved but unafraid.*

LEFT: *A frightened dog holding its tail low between its legs.*

WATCH AND LEARN

Observation is a learned skilled which can be developed by owners. Carefully watch what your dog does when meeting a stranger or another dog and try to interpret the reason behind even seemingly unimportant behaviour. Everything is done for a reason and, with practice, you should be able to identify why your dog does what he does in any given situation.

DOGS FIND WORDS DIFFICULT

Owners also need to appreciate that words are relatively difficult for dogs to learn. Eventually they can learn to associate words with actions, but many repetitions are needed before they understand precisely what is required. It is not a natural method of communication for them and, consequently, owners who rely solely on word commands will find it more difficult to communicate effectively with their dogs.

USING TONE OF VOICE

Dogs will readily determine our mood from our tone of voice. It is not so much what we say, but the way we say it that is important. When talking to your dog, try to modulate the way you say things so that different moods can be conveyed more easily. For example, try to vary the tone of voice used to communicate how urgent a request is, how pleased you are with him, how angry you are, or any other type of feeling you want to get across. Dogs are fairly emotional beings and by communicating our feelings to them more readily,

they will be better able to judge what it is we want from them.

EYE CONTACT

A direct stare between dogs is often used to threaten or intimidate. Since humans often look lovingly into each other's eyes and those of their pets, dogs need to become accustomed to our different use of the same signal. Most dogs will look away when you look into their eyes and begin to look uncomfortable if

LEFT: *Even loving stares from an owner can make a dog feel uncomfortable.*

MIND READING

Most pet dogs study their owner's facial expressions and body language. Consequently, they become expert at reading our moods and seem to know instinctively when we are happy or sad, afraid or cheerful.

you continue to do so. Fearful dogs may growl or back away if you stare. Well-socialized dogs who are familiar with our use of eye contact may stare back happily and wag their tails in greeting.

If you do not know a dog, it is wise to avoid prolonged direct eye contact with him, particularly if you are approaching him. Staring at your own dog may make him feel uncomfortable and this should be avoided. Instead, accustom your dog to eye contact by showing him a titbit and holding it just under your chin. Be patient and wait for him to look up into your eyes. As soon as he does, feed him the food. Your dog will gradually learn to look into your eyes in order to get the titbit. When he

has learned this, you can gradually increase the time for which he looks at you. By doing this you will slowly accustom him to friendly eye contact and make him feel less intimidated by it.

DISPLACEMENT BEHAVIOUR

When dogs feel under pressure or uncomfortable about something, they may carry out a seemingly unrelated, unimportant behaviour, such as yawning, scratching or sniffing. This seems to help them to relieve the anxiety they are feeling and provides a temporary relief from the tension. If your dog does this a lot, you may like to identify what it is that triggers the behaviour. If it is something that you do, you may like to either stop doing it or try to make him feel more comfortable about it in future.

APPEASEMENT GESTURES

Dogs will use a variety of appeasement gestures in response to individuals that they consider to be

LEFT: *Yawning helps to release some of the tension this dog feels.*

higher in status than themselves. These gestures may take the form of lip licking (their own!), skin licking (ours), particularly of the face and mouth, rolling over to expose their vulnerable areas, turning the head away and avoiding eye contact, and urinating. Appeasement gestures help to pacify the more dominant individuals in the pack and reassure them of their status, therefore making it less likely that the subordinate will be attacked. Puppies, juveniles and individuals that consider themselves to be of low status are, therefore, more likely to display such gestures.

Any punishment given by humans in an effort to try to stop these behaviours is likely to have the opposite effect as the dog tries even harder to appease. Understanding the nature of these gestures and attempting to rebuild the dog's confidence and trust are more likely to succeed.

BELOW: *A combination of words and signals will enable a dog to learn commands more easily.*

COMBINING PHYSICAL AND VERBAL SIGNALS

Owners who use a combination of their own body signals and various tones of voice when interacting with their dog, and who are willing to observe and interpret their dog's signals in return, will be able to bridge the species gap in communication more effectively.

CHAPTER THREE

HOW TO BE A GOOD OWNER

Achieving a good relationship between yourself and your dog is one of the most important aspects of dog ownership. A bond of friendship and trust between owner and dog leads to good behaviour and harmony in the household. This can only be achieved if you, as the owner, take the initiative and act in a way that promotes a successful alliance.

YOUR DOG SHOULD WANT TO PLEASE YOU

You can make your dog do what you say, but he will do it reluctantly and because he has to. Having a dog that does things for you willingly is always much more rewarding. This is only possible if you have a relationship with your dog where he genuinely wants to please you because you are his best friend. Such a relationship makes life so much easier and more pleasant for both parties.

The secret to making your dog want to please you lies in making good behaviour advantageous to him. Owners who are able to empathize with their dogs and imagine what it is like to be them are more likely to be successful in achieving good behaviour. Owners who think only of themselves, and what they want, are less likely to be successful.

REWARD GOOD BEHAVIOUR

Whenever your dog does something you approve of, it is important to let him know. If you are his friend, your praise and attention will

LEFT: *Praise from an owner who is also a best friend will mean a lot to a dog.*

mean a lot to him. Give him positive feedback whenever he does something right. This will make him feel happy about doing it and he is more likely to do it again next time. In this way, good behaviour is promoted and is more likely to happen in future.

This may sound too easy and too obvious, but it is surprising how many owners are very quick to reprimand their dog for bad behaviour but ignore him when he is good. Some dogs become so desperate for attention that they prefer being told off to being ignored and their behaviour thus begins to deteriorate. Remembering to reward good behaviour can be more difficult than it seems since your dog will not be drawing attention to himself at this time. It is, however, essential that you make a special effort to do so. Going over to him when he is lying down quietly and gently praising him will make it more likely that he does this more often. Waiting until he has become bored and has begun to chew or whine for attention before responding will make the unwanted behaviour more frequent.

Being affectionate to your dog in this way and providing an environment where you live in harmony most of the time provides a big contrast with times when you may need to reprimand him. If a dog

OPPOSITE: *A good relationship between you and your dog is more fulfilling for both parties.*

has an adversarial relationship with his owner, being told off will be nothing new, but for a dog whose relationship is based on friendship, being told off is a very big deal indeed.

ERROR-FREE LEARNING

Try to manage situations and engineer events so that your dog does the right thing most of the time. This will allow you to be generally positive and rewarding. For example, instead of leaving a young dog alone in the house with nothing to do, provide suitable toys and chews (see page 67) and ensure that he has had a long walk beforehand to tire him out. This will make it less likely that he will get into trouble by chewing things he should not. Providing situations where your dog learns to do the right thing from the outset will be a lot easier than allowing him to get into bad habits which you will then need to break.

PREVENT UNWANTED BEHAVIOUR

Try to think ahead so that you can prevent potential trouble. For example, if you know that your dog has a tendency to jump up on visitors as they arrive, put him on a lead or hold onto his collar before opening the door so that you can prevent him from doing so. You can then praise the good behaviour (even though he had no choice) rather than being forced into the position where you have to reprimand or punish bad behaviour. Physically preventing unwanted behaviour using gentle restraint via a collar and lead will allow good behaviour to happen which can then be rewarded. Allowing too much freedom before you have achieved mental control will mean that your dog will be able to find his own reward in bad behaviour. Once this happens, bad habits begin to form that may be difficult to put right.

BELOW: *Prevent unwanted behaviour by gentle restraint.*

DON'T SHOUT!

Using punishment, scoldings or shouting as a way of stopping bad behaviour is very ineffective. Such measures usually only serve to cause your dog to become worried. Once he is anxious or afraid, he will not be in a good frame of mind to learn the correct way to behave. Rather than learning how to do the right thing next time, your dog learns how unpleasant his owner can sometimes become instead.

When taken to extremes, threats or punishment can intimidate a dog to the point where he becomes frightened to do

BELOW: *Punishing problem behaviour after the event will not prevent it in future.*

anything in case it is wrong. A dog that is frequently punished may live in fear of being attacked by his owners and may begin to bite to defend himself. Since the precise reason for punishment is not always clear, especially if the punishment takes place long after the event that provoked it, owners may often appear, from the dog's point of view, to be unpredictably aggressive. If a dog cannot trust his owners, he is unlikely to trust other humans and, therefore, punishing a dog will make him more likely to bite other people in future.

Constant scoldings and shouting can also be very unpleasant and stressful, for the owner as well as the dog. Not only are they unlikely to produce the desired response from the dog but they also, eventually, destroy a good relationship and can cause resentment. Shouting, particularly, is a sign that the owner is out of control. Only weak, ineffective leaders shout. Strong, efficient leaders only have to make their requirements known to get compliance and, in extreme cases where the dog's desires are very much at odds with those of his owners, they only need to raise their voice slightly to enforce their will. If you often feel the need to shout at your dog, it is probably time to re-evaluate your relationship and build a new one that is based on respect and friendship.

Owners will often punish a dog that has done something wrong while he was left alone. Punishment after the event only serves to increase the dog's view of his owners as unpredictable. Dogs cannot learn from this since they cannot relate the punishment to the unwanted behaviour, even if they are taken to the scene of the crime. They can remember what they have done, just as we can, but they cannot associate the punishment with their earlier behaviour.

Humans are fooled into thinking that they can because their dog will look 'guilty' when they return home. However, this is simply a natural submissive reaction in response to the anger of a pack member of higher status. They may even learn to associate chewed items or mess on the floor with this response and begin to show submission (or look 'guilty') before the

owner has noticed something is amiss. This, unfortunately, provides further evidence of their supposed 'guilt'. Punishing a dog after the event will have no beneficial effect on preventing the behaviour when you are out in future. Again, all it serves to do is to weaken the relationship between you and your dog.

THE NEED FOR A LEADER

Dogs are often much happier and better behaved if they have a strong, supportive leader or leaders to protect and guide them. This frees them from the responsibility of leadership, and they are able to be relaxed and

LEFT: *A submissive reaction to an angry owner – often misinterpreted by us as guilt.*

playful while being safe in the knowledge that someone else is looking after them. Just like young children, dogs prefer to be given direction and guidance, provided that it is not overbearing. Providing them with a framework of guidelines and making the boundaries clear allows them to be sure of their role while maintaining the flexibility to be themselves.

Being a good pack leader is not just about having the right to make the decisions. It is also about taking on the responsibility to protect the pack members and to ensure that their needs are provided for. Your job will be to keep your dog safe and deal with anything he may find threatening, and to provide exercise, games, food and social contact (see Chapter 4). If you meet all of these requirements, your dog will find it very easy to want you as his pack leader and will be loyal and faithful in a way that makes dog ownership worthwhile.

As pack leaders, the way we are feeling will rub off on our

BELOW: *Taking on the pack leader role will allow your dogs to relax and feel safe.*

dogs. If they are closely bonded to us, they will reflect our moods and be influenced by them. If we are anxious, happy, sad or lively, our dogs probably will be too, and this is something to bear in mind during times when you are anxious or stressed. Your dog is likely to pick up on this and become anxious or stressed. Watch out for subtle signs and be aware that behaviour changes in your dog may be a direct result of a behaviour change in you. If possible, stay happy!

DOGS AS PACK ANIMALS

An essential ingredient for all pack animals is to live in a hierarchy in which not all the animals are equal. Hierarchies reduce the risk of injury from fights between the pack members by arranging animals in order of mental and physical strength. Fights only occur between animals of very similar strength and are, therefore, quite rare. Minimizing the fighting in this way is particularly important when individuals possess such large teeth and strong jaws.

Animals at the top of the hierarchy are usually the biggest, strongest and the most clever. They have the right of access to resources in preference to those beneath them in status. In years of famine, a hierarchy ensures that the strongest animals survive to produce the next generation. Since the individuals at the top of the pack are the only ones with the right to breed, competition for the top places is fierce.

Although diluted by the process of

BELOW: *Over a period of time, a natural hierarchy is established among a group of dogs that live together.*

domestication, the desire for high status among our present-day dogs is often a matter of great importance and it is vital that we understand it. Achieving high status means more to some dogs than to others, each individual being different, but, overall, it is a process that is well worth considering when trying to live with a member of a different species in your home.

Having a dog that considers himself below all family members is essential for a harmonious existence. A dog that thinks he is in charge will be very difficult to live with and will want to follow his own ideas instead of those of his owners. He is likely to be over-active, difficult to control, over-boisterous with visitors, and may even be aggressive when he does not get his own way.

HAVING THE RIGHT ATTITUDE

Getting the upper hand is not difficult and there is no need to resort to aggression yourself in order to achieve it. High status, and the respect that goes with it, is something that has to be earned. It is given by the subordinate rather than enforced by the leader. Resorting to punishment may lead to intimidation through fear, but is unlikely to lead to a freely-given

respect for your authority that is so essential for a good relationship. Being a good pack leader is not about bullying others into submission, but about making them want to have you as their leader.

One of the most important qualities for getting respect is to have an air of authority. This is achieved by having the attitude that your dog will be reasonably well behaved and that you will do whatever is necessary to achieve success during your encounters with him. Often it is not the big things that matter, but the smaller, everyday occurrences. It is about insisting, for example, that your dog comes when you call him, or moves out of the way when you ask him. If there are lots of instances where you have won, and he has lost, over smaller issues, he is unlikely to risk bigger challenges as he will not be confident of winning. Therefore, having an attitude that allows you to win small contests will earn you respect from your dog.

Once you have achieved high status, there is no need to keep testing your dog to see if he will give in over small things. If you have won your dog's respect as a leader, he is unlikely to challenge you for your role unless circumstances change dramatically or he is a very strong character. Dogs are often content to let you take the lead provided that you have proved yourself worthy of the role. Usually, they are only too pleased to allow you to take all the responsibility that goes with leadership off their shoulders.

LEARNING TO LEAD THE PACK

In order to be a good pack leader, you need to know which resources your dog considers to be most important. You can then teach your dog that should you require access to these resources at any time, it is your right as pack leader to do so. This is particularly important when taking a puppy or a new adult dog into your pack.

Although you will not need to use these techniques all the time once you have attained leadership status, it is useful to know them so that you can settle a new dog

ABOVE: *Your dog should get out of the chair immediately if you ask him to do so.*

or puppy into your pack more easily. Knowledge of these techniques will also give you a greater understanding of your dog and help you to appreciate why he behaves as he does in certain situations. Resources for dogs fall into four main areas:

FOOD

It is the right of the dominant dog to eat first and to have first choice of any available food. From the point of view of being a strong leader, you should be seen to be eating first if your meals coincide and you should not give up bits of your food to your dog when eating.

SLEEPING PLACES AND TERRITORY

It is the right of the dominant dog to sleep where he wants and to go to or rest in any part of the territory if he wants to. In order to achieve high status, be sure that you are able to remove your dog from the places you want to be whenever you want to be there. Ask him to move if he is blocking the way and, occasionally, ask him to move from where he was resting so that you can sit there yourself. Keep him off beds and chairs if it becomes difficult to remove him easily from them.

As the dominant animal, you should lead the pack and your dog should follow. Make sure that this occurs when going through doorways or narrow passageways together. Those of higher status should always go first.

Height advantage is also important to dogs, and with a new dog or a very

pushy one, you should make sure you keep him below you. This applies to going up or down the stairs, or when you are sitting down.

TOYS AND POSSESSIONS

The dominant dog has the right to make use of any possession within his territory at any time. Usually, the possessions most important to dogs are their toys.

RIGHT: *Strong leaders like to win games and are possessive over toys.*

BELOW: *Being aloof when your dog demands attention can help to raise your status.*

invitations from others if he does not want contact. Not responding to all requests for attention or affection, as well as beginning and ending social interactions to suit you, will confer high status.

WHEN TO SAY 'NO' AND MEAN IT

There will be times when you will need to make it clear to your dog that you are in charge, or times when his behaviour is so unacceptable that you need to ensure that it never happens again. At such a time, use your voice to

To be a strong leader, it is important that you can control games with toys and take possession of them yourself if you want to do so. Playing tug-of-war to win and maintaining possession of the toy at the end of the game is a good way to impress on your dog that you are strong enough to win if you want to.

AFFECTION AND SOCIAL CONTACT
A dominant dog has the right to initiate social interactions if he wishes or ignore

make it obvious that you are not happy. Use a deep, loud exclamation, which is powerful enough to stop your dog in his tracks. Back this up with physical restraint, for example, by holding the dog's collar, to stop the behaviour if necessary, but leave your dog in no doubt that you are displeased.

After such a correction, it is important to get him to do something

EVERY DOG IS DIFFERENT

Some dogs will have stronger characters than others and will need clearer guidelines. Some dogs have such gentle natures that they would not dream of trying to attain a higher station in life, whereas others may push at the boundaries on a regular basis to see if they are still in place. Adolescents, male dogs and dogs from guarding breeds are more likely to push harder than other dogs. Determining the strength of character of your dog and setting limits that are just enough for him to consider you an obvious leader will produce the best outcome for both of you. He will then be free to be himself, but within the boundaries that you have set. Peace and harmony should prevail!

that you can be pleased about. Take him away from the area and ask him to sit or lie down if he knows the command. Give him genuine praise for responding. By providing a contrast between your responses to good and bad behaviour in this way, he will rapidly learn what he should and should not do.

If it becomes obvious that your dog is challenging you for status, as sometimes happens during adolescence or during the early months with a new dog, you will need to make it very obvious that you are stronger than him. Only respond to a challenge if you are willing and able to carry it through and win, no matter what your dog may do. Alternatively, ignore the challenge and ensure that you win over numerous smaller issues, particularly with regard to the resources he finds most important, to reduce his confidence. Work out a strategy to maintain control should a similar challenge arise in future.

LEFT: *Your dog may challenge you but only respond if you are able to win.*

CHAPTER FOUR

ESSENTIAL INGREDIENTS FOR A GOOD DOG

A contented dog is a good dog. Those dogs that do not have everything they need are constantly behaving in ways that make it possible for them to achieve those needs. These ways of behaving are often unacceptable to us and are at odds with how we want our dogs to be. To overcome this, it is necessary to provide for all their essential needs so that they are contented and can relax and behave in an acceptable way.

A dog's essential needs are not that much different from our own. Many owners, however, do not consider that their dogs have any other than those of their physical needs. Keeping their bodies healthy is just one aspect of good dog ownership. Keeping their minds healthy is a different task altogether.

A DOG'S ESSENTIAL NEEDS FOR GOOD MENTAL HEALTH

All essential needs originate from a time when dogs lived as wild animals. In order to fulfil these needs, dogs behave in certain ways. Although there is no longer any necessity to show all of these behaviours for survival, dogs still retain

IMPORTANT BEHAVIOURS FOR DOGS

1 KEEPING SAFE
◆ All safety behaviours, including avoidance, anxiety, defensive and territorial behaviour.

2 BODY MAINTENANCE
◆ Includes all hunting behaviours: running, jumping, digging (play is an acceptable substitute for hunting in modern dogs).
◆ Chewing, eating, protection and storage of food.
◆ Grooming.

3 REPRODUCTION
◆ Behaviours designed to raise and maintain status within the pack (the higher your status, the more likely you are to produce puppies).
◆ Behaviours designed to find a mate.
◆ Mating behaviour.

4 SOCIAL CONTACT (IMPORTANT FOR ALL THREE CATEGORIES ABOVE)
◆ Behaviours designed to enable continued social contact with the rest of the pack.

the capacity and desire to do so. They have four basic needs:

- A need to be safe.
- A need to maintain their bodies.
- A need to reproduce.
- A need for social contact.

A NEED TO BE SAFE

Safety behaviours are all-important. In the wild, if you do not keep safe, you are likely to be injured or killed. This is why feeling

ABOVE: *A happy dog has an owner who caters for all his essential needs.*

safe takes precedence over everything else for our pet dogs. If your dog is stressed, anxious or frightened, he will show a whole range of unwanted behaviours to try to make himself feel more secure.

Dogs today have different fears from those of their ancestors. Dogs get scared of unfamiliar things which appear, to them, to pose a risk to themselves or their pack. Your dog may be frightened of certain people, or all people, of children, delivery people, other dogs, things on wheels, vacuum cleaners, or certain noises. Fear often manifests itself in excessive barking or aggression. It can also cause dogs to be quiet, dull and unresponsive.

Understanding that your dog is fearful, even if he is displaying overt aggression, is essential to solving the problem. Dogs that feel safe in their own world are unlikely to show these unwanted behaviours because there is no need to do so. As an owner, keeping your dog safe from things that frighten him, or helping him to overcome his fear by gradual and repeated exposure to low levels of whatever it is that scares him, will help him to feel safer. By keeping fear levels low and making any new encounters fun (by introducing titbits or games), the problem can be gradually overcome and your dog can feel safe enough to give up displaying the unwanted behaviour.

When a dog finds himself alone, feeling safe is particularly important. Dogs that feel unsafe are likely to try a whole range of behaviours to make themselves feel more secure. They may make frantic attempts to get to their owners and, in doing so, cause damage to doors and windows. Or they may try to surround themselves with their owners' scent and chew things that their owners have recently touched or worn. Alternatively, they may try to dig themselves a den, usually in a sofa or mattress. Or they may decide to mark strategic points with urine to deter anything that may decide to come in and get them while their owners are away.

Isolation is not a natural state for a pack animal. Gradually accustoming your dog to being left alone so that he feels safe when you leave him is essential to good behaviour. Making sure he does not fear other elements of his environment is also necessary. Providing him with a small covered area that resembles a den to hide in, and giving him an item of clothing which smells of you when you leave will also help him to feel safe in your absence.

BELOW: *An open indoor kennel can become a safe den when covered by a thick blanket and placed in a quiet corner.*

A NEED TO MAINTAIN THEIR BODIES

For dogs in the wild, it is essential to stay fit in order to hunt to acquire food. Even though we provide our dogs with all the good quality food they need to survive, they have not lost the desire to stay fit. Providing sufficient physical and mental exercise to fulfil this need is essential if your dog is to be content. Exercising your dog's body only is never enough; exercising his mind is also required.

BELOW: *Running fast after a toy helps to use up a dog's energy.*

WALKING THE DOG

The amount of exercise that a dog needs depends on the individual. Genetics will have an important influence, as will age. Younger dogs from working strains or from breeds that were required to run or work all day will have plenty of energy and will require more exercise. Older dogs or those from breeds designed to be lap dogs will require less exercise. Dogs with bodies that are dictated by fashion to be impractical, such as British Bulldogs or Basset Hounds, will not be able to exercise very much without becoming exhausted.

ABOVE: *Freedom to run and play in a safe area is essential for dogs.*

It is important to provide just the right amount of physical exercise. The consequences of not doing this are obvious. Any excess energy is likely to be channelled into unwanted behaviour, such as over-zealous greeting of owners or visitors, attention-seeking, or very boisterous play with toys or other objects. Living with a dog with too much energy is no joke, and these dogs often get banished to the garden where they annoy the neighbours with excessive barking at the slightest disturbance.

Taking your dog out for walks allows him to use up his energy. Ideally, dogs should be walked at least twice a day – in the morning and evening. This allows them to go to the toilet and exercise physically and mentally. Dogs that are walked away from their homes on a regular basis are less likely to be territorial and are probably more sociable with other animals and people.

The length of time you need to spend out on walks will depend on your dog's energy level. If he is showing unwanted behaviour in the house, you will need to step up the amount he is exercised until you reach a level that suits him. You can increase the amount of exercise he gets on each walk by playing games with him. Remember to take his toys out with you rather than playing with sticks which can

ABOVE: *A tired but contented dog after some stimulating and energetic exercise with his owner.*

injure him. You can also increase the amount of exercise he gets by letting him off the lead to run free. For all dogs, freedom off the lead to run and play is essential. Ensure that your dog is under control, by teaching him to come back reliably when called (see page 82).

MIND GAMES

Dogs evolved from a species that needed to hunt to survive. When man first domesticated them, he bred them to do specific jobs and gave them plenty of work to do. Now, pet dogs have no job other than to entertain us. So often, loving owners provide everything their dog needs to keep his body healthy but expect him to lie around the house all day while they get on with their busy lives. This may suit some dogs, but not the majority, especially those that were bred to have the mental strength and stamina to work all day.

In the absence of hunting or work to do, dogs need an outlet for all the mental energy they have. Games with toys help to do this, providing an outlet for both physical and mental energy and, in addition, a way of strengthening the bond between you and your dog. Dogs that are playing with their owners are not getting into trouble with other dogs in the park, chasing livestock or running away from home to find more excitement. Dogs that play with their owners are likely to be more sociable and more in tune with people generally.

Try to play with your dog as often as possible. It is better to split up a long play session into several shorter ones that occur periodically throughout the day. In this way, your dog will have something to look forward to and you can use the play sessions as a reward for good behaviour. Playing outside in the garden or on walks will release more physical energy, but you will need also to invent games that can be played inside during bad weather. Teaching your dog to play 'hide and seek' games with toys, or other

BELOW: *Games with toys tire the mind as well as the body.*

games that require you to put in just minimum effort, will make it more likely that you will choose to play them more often (see opposite).

All dogs enjoy playing but some don't know how to play with toys and need to be taught. Begin with soft toys, which they will enjoy holding in their mouths, and keep them moving fast and erratically. Concentrate on the toy rather than your dog and be as exciting and child-like as possible. Encourage any move the dog

makes towards the toy and keep sessions short at first to ensure that he is still interested next time. You may find that putting food inside the toy encourages his interest and makes it more likely that he will try to grab it. Building up the ability to play in this way takes time, but it is well worth it for the benefits it brings.

In addition to playing games, by training your dog, teaching him tricks and to be useful around the house (see Chapter 7), you will tire him. A dog that lives his life with you, goes out often and accompanies you on excursions will be using up his mental energy and, as a result, will be better behaved. In comparison, a dog that is kept mostly in the kitchen or garden and only taken out occasionally is likely to have too much energy to control and will be very difficult to live with and take out.

Left: Many dogs enjoy tugging games.
Adults should supervise children and
help them to win if necessary.

DIFFERENT TYPES OF GAMES— DOGS WITH THEIR OWNERS

Different dogs enjoy different types of games. There are two types of interactive games that we can play with our dogs.

CHASE GAMES

These are enjoyed by the majority of dogs, particularly those from the herding breeds. Let your dog chase the toy; do not chase after him. Teach him to retrieve toys (see page 100) so that he brings them back to you to throw again.

TUGGING GAMES

These games are enjoyed by dogs from the guarding breeds, Boxers, Bull Terriers, and dogs with a strong possessive

ABOVE: *Most dogs enjoy chase games, particularly collies and herding dogs.*

character. It is advisable to win more often than you lose and to take the toy away with you at the end of the game. This will insure that your dog always thinks you are stronger than him.

DIFFERENT TYPES OF GAMES— DOGS ON THEIR OWN

There are three types of games we can set up for our dogs to play by themselves.

SEARCHING GAMES

These are enjoyed by all dogs once they have learned how to play. Teach your dog how to find hidden objects by rolling toys

into long grass and then releasing the dog with a "find" command. Develop this game over time until he can find a hidden object in any area.

DIGGING GAMES

These are enjoyed by Terriers or dogs from breeds bred to go to ground, such as the Dachshund. Create a visually marked area to be used as a digging pit and teach your dog to find buried bones and chews there.

GAMES WITH SQUEAKY TOYS

These are enjoyed by Terriers and other dogs with a strong predatory instinct. How determined your dog is to kill the squeak will give you an indication of how strong his predatory nature is. Dogs that like squeaky toy games will often enjoy

ABOVE: *Digging is often frantic if a dog can hear or smell small animals burrowing beneath the surface.*

catching and killing small animals. For dogs that are overexcited by this game, it is not advisable to play it excessively.

NO BITING ALLOWED

If your dog's teeth make contact with your hands during games, even if it was accidental, draw his attention to it by yelping as if in pain and end the game. This will teach him to be very careful with his teeth in any future games.

A TOY FOR EVERY OCCASION

There are many different toys on the market. Choose ones that you think you and your dog will enjoy playing with and that suit the type of game your dog likes to play. For dogs that are more interested in food than games, choose toys that have holes in them into which you can squeeze dog biscuits, treats, or cheese. This will help to increase their interest in toys and make it much more likely that they will enjoy playing with them.

CHEWING

Food for our pet dogs hardly needs to be chewed at all. Food for their ancestors, however, came in the form of entire carcasses and required a great deal of chewing. Even though it is now no longer necessary, domestic dogs have retained the desire to chew and will do so throughout their lives. We need to provide them with suitable items to insure that they have an outlet for this behavior. Failure to do so can result in our dogs chewing things we would rather they did not.

Young dogs, especially those going through puppyhood or between the ages of six and ten months, tend to chew the most. Suitable items to give them include anything that can be chewed that will not cause injury. Items that dogs are most enthusiastic about chewing are usually edible. Large marrowbones, rawhide chews, or similar types of by-products are all suitable. Strong toys can also be stuffed with food which has to be licked and chewed out by your dog. Try to provide a variety of chews so that a new, interesting one appears every so often. Make sure that there are always a few suitable items available. This will insure that he will not eat to excess, as sometimes happens when chews or bones are given only rarely, and that he is less likely to guard the objects given.

A NEED TO REPRODUCE

In a wolf pack, only those at the top of the hierarchy are likely to breed and, consequently, achieving high status is very important to them. The ambition to be the top dog has been retained to a lesser extent in our pet dogs, although more so in some than in others. Since our dogs look upon us as their pack, achieving high status in the family can be important to them. Impressing on your dog that his place is definitely at the bottom of the pack (see Chapter 3) will satisfy him that he has done all he can to get as high as he can and he will, hopefully, give up trying.

Competition for the right to breed can often become a problem among pet dogs if two or more unneutered males or unspayed females are kept together. If they have similar strengths of character, they are likely to compete between themselves. This becomes particularly noticeable during seasons in females and whenever the males can smell the scent of a bitch in heat. If bitches are kept together, it is advisable to have them spayed to eliminate problems due to fluctuating hormone levels at times when they are in season (or in heat). Since males do not have

seasons and are competing with each other throughout the year, it may be beneficial to neuter both of the dogs to eliminate the gap between them in terms of status. Although this may go against the desire of owners to neuter both pets, it is actually better for the dogs as they can then accept their positions more easily.

The desire to mate is stronger in some dogs than in others. Some males will pace up and down, lose weight, and make frantic attempts to get to bitches in season, while others are not so interested. Dogs that have a strong desire to mate will often compete with other male dogs in their neighborhood and will mark their territory and spend a lot of time sniffing lampposts and other dogs. They are the sort who will often try to escape, run away from home, and spend time roaming, looking for a mate. They may also attempt to mount bedding, stuffed toys, children, or people's legs. Such dogs usually benefit from being neutered. This relatively simple surgical operation can save them years of frustration and removes the unwanted behavior that is caused by their hormones.

A NEED FOR SOCIAL CONTACT

All members of a social species need contact with others to thrive, and dogs are no exception. In the wild, being a member of a pack is a fundamental requirement for staying safe and healthy. Our domestic dogs also need to feel that they are closely associated with the other members of their pack, and, since they often live only with people, staying friends with their human family is very important to them.

Providing love and attention may seem an obvious task but, for many dog owners, the role of their pet dog is to provide them with love and attention, not necessarily the other way around. Some owners are just too busy or too stressed by caring for other members of the family, particularly if they have young children, to have anything left for their dog. Deprived of good-quality love and attention from their owners, dogs become desperate to get a response of any kind and can resort to disruptive and even troublesome behavior.

Try to provide your dog with at least five minutes that you set aside just for him several times a day. This may not seem like much, and you can certainly give more time if you have it, but these few minutes of undivided attention will mean a great deal to him. During this time you can stroke him, talk to him, or give him whatever kind of attention he finds most enjoyable. The important thing is to make him feel loved and wanted. He needs to know that he is getting your undivided attention, that you are not doing it as a chore, but that you genuinely want to spend time with him.

Giving him quality time in this way will help him to feel connected to you and that he is part of the pack. This will allow him to feel safe and secure and will help prevent many of the unwanted behaviors that occur when dogs feel isolated and distanced from their pack.

CHAPTER FIVE

HOW AND WHY DOGS LEARN

A popular misconception is that, as the owner, you have the right to expect obedience from your dog. However, dogs do not come ready-programmed to obey. They are opportunistic individuals and will do whatever is to their advantage at any given moment. If we want them to do as we ask, we not only need to teach them the commands for certain actions but must also make it worthwhile for them to comply with our requests.

WHY USE REWARDS?

The fundamental principle behind learning in all animals is that behavior and actions that are rewarded will happen more often. A dog that has overturned a trash can and found something tasty inside, for example, is likely to do it again, or a dog that jumps up and is given attention is likely to do so whenever he greets someone he likes.

In a similar way, words associated with rewarding experiences are

RIGHT: *Dogs are happy to learn if it is in their interests to do so.*

also remembered. Think how quickly a dog learns the word "walk!" or "cookie!" If we can get that kind of enthusiasm associated with the words "down" or "come" by using rewards, training will be easy.

Once your dog knows the commands, he will often be happy to work for just your praise if he has a good relationship with you. However, in the early stages of training when he does not know what you want, he will have to work much harder in order to comply with your requests. During this time, a pet dog that gets praise for free most of the time is likely to need other inducements to encourage him to comply.

Once your dog knows your signals, there will be times when your requests are in direct conflict with what he wants to do (for example, if you have just called him when he is playing with another dog, or he wants to lie down and rest and you want him to do obedience exercises). At these times, the value of the reward you are offering needs to be higher than the rewards he would get if he did what he wanted to do.

MOTIVATION FOR OBEDIENCE

To make it easier for you to encourage your dog to comply with your requests, you will need to know what motivates him. Although there are several areas of interest for dogs, it should be remembered that they are all individuals and what interests one may not interest another. Finding out what your dog really likes from the list below is necessary before you can begin training:

1 Praise and attention
2 Food
3 Games and play
4 Movement

1 PRAISE AND ATTENTION

If you are part of your dog's pack, he will want to stay friends with you. If you are of a higher status, he will choose to obey you because he will have respect for you. The higher he perceives your status to be, the more likely it is that he will comply with your requests. If you are finding it difficult to keep control and he is often disobedient, even though you think he knows the signals, you may need to increase your status using the methods given in Chapter 3.

If you have a good relationship with your dog, he will want to please you and will enjoy your praise and attention. You

BELOW: *Children are often very good at motivating dogs, as they are enthusiastic, genuine, and uninhibited.*

should remember, however, that pet dogs often get lots of praise and attention just for being there and, because of this, they may not be as willing to work for it. If you are constantly giving your dog attention because you want to, you may need to use other inducements to get him to work for you. Alternatively, you may want to reduce the amount of free attention you give and ask your dog to do something to earn it in the future.

There are several ways to give attention. It is important to choose the way that your dog enjoys the most.

◆ TALKING

Praise your dog in a high-pitched, happy tone of voice. Let him know you are genuinely pleased when he has done something right and make this tone of voice very different from any other that you use. Be unrestrained and extravagant in your praise so that he is left in no doubt that he has pleased you. Children often praise very well because they are less restrained than adults and giggle and squeal excitedly, which makes it fun for the dog too.

◆ LOOKING

Some dogs will enjoy direct eye contact more than others. If it makes your dog feel uncomfortable, do not stare at him while you praise him but look at his tail instead.

◆ TOUCHING

Some dogs like to be touched more than others. If your dog finds it rewarding, make contact with him when he has done

AIM FOR SUCCESS

During the training process, particularly with a young or adolescent dog, do not give commands that cannot be enforced (e.g., do not give him the signal to come if he is off the lead, half a field away, and running after a rabbit). Instead, only give commands when you are in a position to make your dog comply if he does not respond. Give just one command and ensure that you do something about it if your dog does not respond. It is probably best to assume that he did not understand and to lure or guide him into the required action so you can then praise him. If you do this every time you ask him to do something, he will learn that he has little choice but to comply. If, instead, you often give commands that he ignores and you do not back it up with action, he will become desensitized to your voice and unresponsive.

something right. Dogs have different body sensitivities and preferences, so it is important that you find out how and where your dog likes to be touched. Some prefer you not to touch their heads but like to be stroked under the chin. Others prefer to be touched along the back instead. Most dogs enjoy being stroked on the chest area. Whether you pat, stroke, or tickle should be decided by your dog.

2 FOOD

Most dogs can be motivated by food, particularly those with large appetites, such as Labradors. They do not have to be hungry to do so, although it is advisable

to arrange training sessions to coincide with times when your dog is about to be fed. The amount of food given each time needs to be small so that the dog does not become full too quickly. Strangely, dogs seem to work harder for smaller pieces of food than for larger ones. The more aromatic and tasty the food, the more interested they will be. For convenience, it helps to use dried food. Pieces of cooked, roasted liver no bigger than the size of a pea are ideal.

You may find that your dog becomes bored with the treats you are using after a

RIGHT: *Rewards in the form of tasty tidbits and gentle praise make it more likely that your dog will repeat the behavior.*

LESSONS AWAY FROM HOME

Once you begin to work in areas other than in your home surroundings, you may notice that your dog becomes disinterested in the reward you are offering. There are two possible reasons. One is that the motivation to explore new surroundings or play with other dogs is greater, or it could be that your dog finds it slightly stressful in the outside world and is too anxious to play or eat. Take time to let him get used to the surroundings and either become bored with them or less anxious. Only then will he begin to pay attention to you and the rewards you have to offer.

while. Change to something else, such as small squares of hard cheese, and you should see an improvement. Using a variety of different treats on a regular basis will help to prevent this problem.

3 GAMES AND PLAY

One of the best ways to motivate your dog to do things for you is through games. Games make learning fun and if your dog is having fun he is more likely to remember the lessons. Choose the game your dog likes the most (see page 65) and use it to encourage and reward the desired action.

4 MOVEMENT

Although it is difficult to use as a reward for the desired behavior, it should be remembered that movement is often intrinsically rewarding to dogs, especially young, energetic ones. Being allowed to run free or move forward rather than stand still will be rewarding for them.

SHORT TRAINING SESSIONS

Aim to train in very short sessions of less than five minutes' duration. Several of these throughout the day on walks and at home, while you wait for the kettle to boil, or during commercial breaks, or when you have some free time in the evening, will soon result in a well-trained dog. As the sessions will be short, your dog will remain interested and keen to work. Long sessions result in tired, bored dogs and owners. At the end of each session, you should see some progress in terms of what your dog has learned. If not, think carefully about what you are trying to teach him and the way you are doing it. Training a dog requires lots of thought by the owner to achieve success. Try to think in between sessions about how to teach your dog and what he is learning rather than during the session when you should be concentrating on him.

If you cannot get your dog to do what you want, you are likely to get frustrated. Anger is a natural consequence of frustration. If you find yourself becoming angry, then ask your dog to do something that you know he can do so that you can reward him and immediately end the training session. Take time to calm down and think about what is going wrong so that your dog is more likely to get it right next time.

Dogs, like us, have days when they are feeling off color. If your dog is not in top form on any one day, give him a rest and resume training the next day. Before you begin a training session, you must insure that your dog is not exercised too much or too little and has had the opportunity to go to the bathroom.

Dogs will not be able to concentrate or learn as quickly if they are stressed or worried. This is why it is important not to punish them in any

way if they do not get things right. Just ignore incorrect moves or prevent them with some gentle restraint, and be sure to reward the right action.

RIGHT: *Keeping a supply of treats around the house will enable you to do many short training sessions whenever you have a spare moment.*

TEACHING WORDS AND SIGNALS

Teaching a command can be broken down into three parts. You need to do the following:
◆ Get your dog to do the required action.
◆ Reward the desired action so it is more likely to happen in the future.
◆ Associate a command with the required action.
All of the above require patience in order to achieve the desired behavior, and many repetitions to insure success.

GETTING THE REQUIRED ACTION—LURES VERSUS POSITIONING

In order to achieve the action that you require, it is best to lure your dog into position using a reward, or carefully position the reward so that he has to perform the required action to get it. This

SIGNALS OR WORDS?

Hand signals will be learned much more readily than spoken words. To help your dog to learn the words, it may be beneficial to teach him using both a hand signal and a word, gradually reducing the hand signal as he becomes more experienced until only the word is left.

method is very successful because the dog is thinking about the situation and coming up with the idea of what to do all by himself. As the dog begins to understand what is required, the reward needs to be concealed so that it is not acting as such an obvious enticement. In this way, the dog becomes less fixated on the reward itself and is more likely to pay attention to any signals being given. Eventually, the lure can be dispensed with altogether as the dog begins to respond to the signal only.

The other method of achieving the required action is to position the dog manually, thereby leaving him no choice but to carry out the behavior you want. Although this method does get results as the dog begins to associate the required behavior with the command, it is often slower because the dog is not thinking for himself but is instead distracted by the feeling of being pulled or pushed. In addition, if too much force is used, or he is apprehensive of being handled, positioning him in this way may cause him anxiety that may interfere with his ability to learn.

TIMING

Dogs live in the present, not the past or future, and need to be rewarded for good behavior immediately rather than later. They can remember what they have done, but without language we cannot specify which particular behavior the reward is for. Therefore, to make any difference to future actions, rewards have to be given immediately. Even more than two seconds later is too late because your dog will already be thinking of something else.

For the best results, begin to reward with praise as soon as your dog begins the required action and back this up with other rewards as he completes it.

PUTTING THE ACTION ON COMMAND

Once you are able to make your dog do the desired action, you will want to put it on cue so that it will happen when you signal. In order to do this, all that is necessary is to signal to your dog just before the required action occurs so that he can associate it with the desired response.

For example, if you are teaching your dog to sit and have been luring him into position so that he will sit whenever you raise a tidbit above his head, you will need to begin saying "sit" just before you begin to raise the tidbit. He will then begin to associate the word with the action of putting his bottom on the floor.

Many repetitions of this will be necessary before your dog begins to anticipate what you want from him and he begins to do the action before being

UNREWARDING BEHAVIOR

Actions that are not rewarded are less likely to be repeated. When we attempt to train a dog, we need to insure that unwanted behavior or action is not rewarded accidentally. Since some of these actions, such as moving away from a stay, are often rewarding in themselves, we need to be one step ahead and prevent them from happening at all.

lured into position. When he begins to understand what you mean, you will need to leave a slightly longer gap between the signal and luring him into position to give him time to act on his own.

ASSOCIATIONS

When your dog begins to work out what to do to get the reward, he will learn a set of associations surrounding the event. If you change any of these associations, he will need to be taught the lesson from the beginning again. For example, if you teach him to sit in the kitchen and then take him to the backyard and ask him to sit, he will not necessarily know what you mean. This is because he has learned a response to a set of associations, such as standing in front of you, the signal for "sit," facing the sink, and being next to the table. If you remove all of these except two, i.e., standing in front of you and the signal for "sit," he may find it difficult to work out what you mean. To overcome this, you will need to teach him the lesson from the beginning in many different places and with him, and you, in many different positions until he begins to link the action to the signal only.

BELOW: *At first, dogs learn a set of associations rather than the command only. Teaching your dog to sit when he is in front of you, and then beside you, will help him to learn the command by itself.*

TRAINING CLASSES

Only take your dog to training classes that use kind, reward-based methods. Ask your veterinarian to refer you to the nearest dog training school or classes which use kind, fair, and effective methods. Avoid classes that use choke chains or reprimands. It is sensible to go along to the class without your dog at first so that you can see what goes on before you make your decision. A good class with nothing to hide will welcome this approach. If dogs and owners are happy and are progressing, then sign up, but be prepared to search to find a class that is suitable.

CHAPTER SIX

USEFUL TRAINING EXERCISES

Teaching your dog to come back when called, to walk without pulling on the lead, and to sit, lie down, stand, and roll over on command will make life easier for both of you. A dog that understands these commands and responds readily is likely to be taken out more often and given more freedom than a dog that does not respond appropriately.

BELOW: *Teaching your dog to sit gives you more control and better behavior, especially when your dog is off his lead.*

COMING BACK WHEN CALLED

Coming back when called is an essential command that will enable you to call your dog away from danger once you let him off the lead. It is one of the most useful commands a pet dog ever learns. Having a dog that reliably comes when called allows you to give him more freedom and more exercise. This will make him more contented and, ultimately, better behaved.

1 Get someone to hold your dog by his collar. Show him that you have something that he wants.

2 Run backward, stop, and crouch down facing toward him. Call him enthusiastically while opening your arms in a welcoming gesture (at this point, your helper should release his collar).

3 As he comes toward you, praise him in high, squeaky tones. As he gets closer, offer him the reward and use it to lure him right up to you. Before giving the reward, hold on to his collar. Give the reward but, before letting go of his collar, make a mental connection with him by praising him enthusiastically and letting him know he has done well.

◆ Practice this training exercise over several sessions until your dog begins to understand what you mean. At this point, you can dispense with your helper and call your dog when he is thinking of something else. Remember to use the same words each time and to call in the

WHEN NOT TO CALL

Never call your dog when you want to do something with him that he may find unpleasant, such as bathing him, cutting his nails, or shutting him away from company, as it will make him less willing to respond next time. Always go and get him instead.

DOGS THAT PREFER GAMES

2

If you are using a game with a toy as a reward rather than a tidbit, briefly hold his collar and then play enthusiastically.

same tone of voice. Stop using the food or toy as a lure once he is coming to you readily and, instead, give it as a reward when he gets to you. Remember to praise him genuinely and enthusiastically every time he responds.

3

◆ It is best to begin teaching this exercise in your house or backyard where there are few distractions. Keep a supply of tidbits or toys handy in various places and practice it frequently throughout the day. Use anything that your dog finds interesting as a reward for coming, such as games, tidbits, his dinner, and going out for a walk.

◆ When your dog is coming to you enthusiastically as soon as he hears your call, whether he is in sight or not, begin

to practice outside on a walk. To start with, choose a place where there are no distractions, such as other dogs, children,

ABOVE: Some dogs are more interested in games than tidbits. Use whatever your dog enjoys most.

or traffic. Unless you are in a securely fenced area, attach a line to his collar so that he cannot run off and so that you can enforce the command if necessary. (Be careful not to get tangled in the line. You may find it easier to use a flexi-lead at first, particularly if you have a large, boisterous dog.) Remember to call in the same light-hearted way as you did when you called your dog for his dinner at home and to reward and praise him enthusiastically when he responds.

◆ Call him three or four times on each walk and remember to reward him well with something he really likes when he comes to you. Hold his collar while you reward him and immediately let him run off again so that he learns that coming to you does not signify the end of his freedom. In the early stages, try to call him only when he is heading in your direction or when he looks as though he is slightly bored with what he is doing. Aim for success every time so that your dog learns to respond rapidly rather than to ignore your call.

◆ When he is coming to you as soon as you call, you will need to practice getting the same enthusiastic response when he is thinking of other things. While he is quite close to you but is distracted by a smell in the grass, or has just seen another dog in the distance, call him excitedly and reward him well if he comes. If he does not, use the line to reinforce your command, while running backward and calling excitedly to make it more fun to run to you. You may need to use better rewards at this stage (i.e., his favorite toy or more appetizing food). Practice this many times, gradually stepping up the intensity of the distraction and the distance your dog is away from you.

◆ When you are getting an immediate, enthusiastic response in the presence of distractions while he is some distance from you, it will be safe to let him off the lead. Choose a quiet safe area at first and allow him to run free for a while before calling him back. Reward him well and let him go again. Call him back whenever he gets too far away from you so that he is always under your control.

◆ Never tell him off when he comes to you. Always try to be as enthusiastic and rewarding as you can—no matter what he has just done!

KEEP HIM GUESSING

Once your dog has learned to come back when called, vary the reward you give so that he is kept guessing as to what it might be, i.e., sometimes give one piece of food, sometimes a game with a toy, sometimes a heap of really tasty food and an enthusiastic game. Randomizing rewards in this way will keep him interested and make his response more rapid. Save the best rewards for the best responses so that these are encouraged.

WALKING WITHOUT PULLING ON THE LEAD

This is another essential lesson since dogs that pull on the lead are unpleasant to take out and frequently get left at home. Dogs that are a pleasure to walk are taken out more frequently and get more exercise.

The secret to making a dog walk on the lead without pulling is to move forward only when the lead is slack and to stop when the lead is taut. This sounds very simple, but it is often the opposite of what actually happens between most dogs and their owners. Dogs rapidly learn that leaning into the collar causes their owner to move forward. From there, walking on a lead easily falls into the pattern of the dog pulling and the owner moving forward. Owners often stop their dog when they get fed up, which results in the dog temporarily giving up the struggle, but he soon begins to pull again as soon as it is safe to do so.

To break this pattern, it is important to be consistent. Make a fresh start and, from now on, make an agreement with all members of the family that no one allows the dog to pull

USE HUMANE METHODS

Never use "choke" chains or other similar devices which are designed to stop a dog pulling. They can cause discomfort and long-term damage to the dog's neck. Using an ordinary collar and lead is just as effective and more humane.

on the lead. The technique for walking on a slack lead is as follows.

First, insure that you have the right equipment. A strong buckle collar is needed. Attach a lead which, if your dog were standing beside you with it clipped to his

CANINE HEAD COLLARS

An easy way to prevent pulling is to use a canine head collar. Products like this type of collar allow you to control your dog's head and work on the same principle as head collars for horses. Where his head goes his body will follow and it is much more difficult for him to pull you along than if he has something around his neck.

collar, would allow you to hold the handle against your stomach while the rest of the lead falls in a nice loop which does not quite reach the floor. Anything shorter than this will not allow your dog enough freedom, while anything longer will get tangled up.

1 Clip your dog's lead on and stand still, holding the handle of the lead into your stomach with both hands. If he pulls into the lead, give the lead short, sharp tugs so that he cannot rely on it to support him. This will cause him to stand up

straight rather than to lean into the lead. Do not say anything as this will confuse both him and you and break the concentration. Once he is standing without leaning, the lead should fall slack. As soon as this happens, you can move forward.

2 If he bounds ahead, causing the lead to become tight, hold the lead tightly into your stomach and stand still. (If he runs forward at speed, lean back slightly in anticipation of the jolt that will happen as you cause him to stop.) Always try to anticipate the lead becoming tight so that

you stop just before it does so. In this way, your dog will find that he gets a sharp tug on the lead when he gets a certain distance from you and, worse still, he has to stop when he wants to go forward.

3 Make him stand up straight again so that the lead goes slack by giving short, sharp tugs. Move forward only when the lead is slack. If he runs around or behind you, stop. Maneuver him so that he is back in position and begin again.

4 Repeat stage 3 until he begins to concentrate on keeping the lead slack.

When he is doing so, praise him quietly and tell him how good he is.

There is no need to give any other rewards since the movement of going forward is a reward in itself. It may take a long time to get your dog to walk without pulling initially, but you will progress faster as he begins to learn what is required and break with old habits. He is likely to forget himself when he gets excited, but go back to your new routine if he pulls and he will soon learn that it is not in his interests to do so.

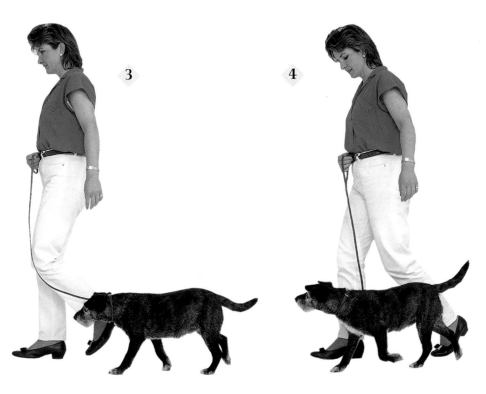

3

4

SIT, DOWN, STAND, AND ROLL OVER

It is useful to have a set of words to tell your dog which positions you want him to take up. This allows you to deal with him easily when necessary, for example, when a visitor who is frightened of dogs enters your house and you want your dog to sit down, or when the veterinarian needs to examine him underneath.

Choose the words you want to use for the various positions and keep to them. It is also useful to decide on a temporary hand signal that will help your dog to learn the appropriate word.

SIT

1 Use food to lure your dog into the required position. Hold a tidbit firmly between your thumb and finger just above his nose.

2 He will raise his nose to try to eat the tidbit and you need to move the tidbit in such a way that he continues to raise his nose in a backward direction.

3 As his head goes up and back, his bottom is likely to go down into the sit position as he attempts to balance himself. When it does so, feed the tidbit and praise him enthusiastically. Keep praising while he maintains the position and stop when it is time for him to get up.

◆ This command sounds simple, but it does require some patience to achieve initially. As your dog begins to work out what is required it will get easier. It may be helpful to back him up against a wall so that he cannot just run backward as you try to do this. Dogs that have been previously trained by being positioned may also respond to gentle pressure on their hindquarters, but if this does not work, revert to using the food lure method as described.

◆ Gradually, your dog will begin to understand what is required and will start

1

to sit down as you move the tidbit over his head. When this happens, start to give the "sit" command just before you move your hand toward him so that he can begin to make the association between the word and his action. Practice this over many short sessions.

◆ Once your dog is automatically sitting as you hold a tidbit up to his nose, conceal the tidbit in your hand. Eventually you will be able to make the action of approaching his nose with the tidbit into a hand signal. Continue to practice, always giving the command just before the hand signal and gradually reducing the hand signal until just the word remains.

"SIT DOWN"

Be careful about saying "sit down" when asking your dog to sit. Use "sit" for sit and "down" for down. If you say "sit down," your dog is likely to respond to the last command he hears and will end up lying down instead of sitting.

◆ Practice in a variety of different places with your dog in many different positions relative to you.

2

3

DOWN

1 In a similar way, use a tidbit to lure your dog into position. First, get him into a sit position.

2 Bring the tidbit down between his front paws. It will take patience at first, but persevere, keeping all hand movements slow and deliberate. He will soon learn how to respond.

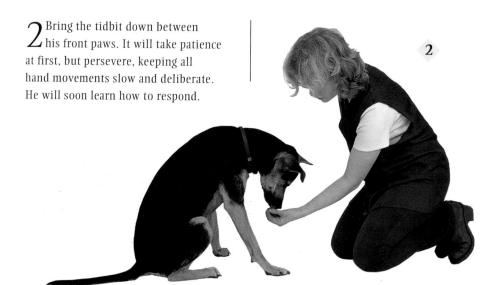

3 If your dog has tried many times to get the tidbit and is getting fed up, give him the odd piece of food just for lowering his head to keep him interested. If he stands up, get him back into a sit position and try again.

4 As soon as he begins to lie down, praise him, then feed him the tidbit and praise him profusely when his elbows touch the ground.

◆ When your dog begins to respond to the food lure and starts to understand what he must do to get the food, begin to give your command just prior to your hand reaching out to him.

◆ In the same way as for the sit, you should practice this command many times in short sessions. Begin to conceal the food and develop the hand signal, and finally phase out the hand signal to leave just the word. Practice in a variety of different places and with him in different positions relative to you.

STAND

1 This is achieved in a similar way to the sit and down. From the sit position, lure the dog's head forward by moving the tidbit away from him in line with his nose until he has to get up to reach the tidbit.

2 As he gets up, keep the tidbit still and reward him well when he is in position. Use the same techniques as for the sit and down to teach the command for the stand.

◆ Due to the way in which dogs learn a set of associations, you should keep in mind that if you teach your dog to stand from the sitting position, he will not understand you if you ask him to stand from the down position. You will need to teach him all over again from the down position if you want him to understand the word properly.

ROLL OVER

1 Once you have achieved a good, instant down, kneel down beside your dog and hold the tidbit so that it is at the side of his nose.

2 As he turns his head to reach it, move the tidbit alongside his face and back toward his collar so that he has to twist his head to reach the tidbit while keeping it very close to his body.

3 As he does so, your dog should roll over onto his side.

◆ Your dog will need to be very relaxed to do this and it is helpful if he is lying on something soft. Practice this until he understands what he needs to do. Eventually you should be able to roll him right over without touching him as he follows your hand around. Use the same techniques as for the sit and down to teach a command for this action.

STAY

Having a dog who will reliably stay in a place where you have put him can be useful on numerous occasions in daily life. It is relatively easy to teach, but it takes time to make him reliable in times of excitement.

1 Begin with your dog in the sit beside you. Give him a hand signal (an obvious one is the flat of your hand held in front of his face for a second) and tell him to stay. Stand next to him without moving and praise him for staying put.

Try to anticipate any movement and correct him, using the lead and collar, if he tries to move. If he gets up, replace him in the same place, repeat the command and the hand signal and praise him after a few moments when he stays still. Reward him for staying still while he is in position. Release him with a separate command (such as "OK") to bring the exercise to an end and ignore him as he moves off. In this way he will learn that he gets rewarded for staying still, but no rewards for moving. Practice this often, gradually building up the

RIGHT: *Continue the training in different places with varying levels of distraction until you have a reliable response.*

time he stays in place until he is happy to stay sitting for five minutes.

2 When your dog will stay still while you stand beside him, begin to move away from him by taking one small step away from him. Correct him immediately if he moves, and praise him if he stays still. In this way, gradually build up to moving further away from him over several sessions.

3 When he is happy to sit still while you walk around him, begin to build up the level of distractions that are happening around him. Eventually, you can also practice asking him to stay when he really wants to do something else.

PRACTICED BUT NOT PERFECT

Practicing in this way will gradually make your dog more reliable. However, no dog can be trusted completely, so never leave him in a "sit stay" outside a shop or near a busy road or anywhere he may be in danger.

3

HOW TO MAKE YOUR DOG REALLY CLEVER

Teaching your dog how to do things above and beyond the normal training routines brings benefits that few owners realize. It strengthens the bond between the dog and his owner and creates a relationship that is based on understanding and friendship. Life becomes more fun and more enjoyable for your dog. The benefits to you are that your dog will be better behaved, can be useful, and is a pleasure to have around.

Once you have mastered the basic training exercises, it will be quite easy to teach what follows. Dogs, like humans, become better at learning the more they do something. As they become educated, and your skill at teaching them grows, it will become easier and easier to teach your dog new things.

BELOW: *Once you have taught your dog the basic lessons, you can begin to teach him creative exercises and games which will make life more fun for you both.*

THE RETRIEVE

This exercise is the foundation on which
many games and tricks are built and is
essential if you want to educate your
dog further. There are many ways to teach
the retrieve, and which one is right for
you will depend on your dog's previous
experience. The basic method is given
here, which is easy to learn. Before
beginning this exercise, your dog will
need to be very interested in playing with
toys (see Chapter 4).

1 Choose a quiet, familiar place, such
as the backyard, and try to choose a
time when your dog is ready to play.
Attach a long piece of thin line to your
dog's collar. Clothesline is ideal for this,
as it is light and does not tangle easily.
This should trail along the ground behind
your dog (for this reason, you should not
use a flexi-lead).

2 Present his favorite toy, wave it
in front of him enthusiastically, and
tease him with it for a few moments.
When he becomes excited and attempts
to join in the game, throw the toy so
that he can follow where it has gone and
so that it moves fast and lands not too
far away from you.

Encourage him to go to it and pick
it up, giving your signal for retrieving,
such as saying "fetch" excitedly and
enthusiastically. Keep this lighthearted
and make the toy move again if necessary
to excite him.

3 When he has the toy in his mouth, do not move toward him. If you move away from him, he is more likely to come to you. Pick up the end of the line attached to his collar and call him to you. If he does not come, or comes a little way and stops, encourage him to come closer by gentle tugs on the line and by running backward. Praise him enthusiastically as he comes closer. (If he drops the toy at

this stage, quickly encourage him to "fetch" again.)

4 When he gets close to you, do not reach out to touch him or the toy as this will make him want to avoid you in the future so he can keep his toy. Instead, praise him quietly and stroke him on his back when he is close enough. (If he drops the toy at this stage, encourage him to pick it up again by nudging it forward and asking him to "fetch.")

5 When he has been holding the toy for a few moments, quietly reach out, take the toy from him, and repeat the above stages. If your dog's favorite game is tug-of-war, play this game with the toy for a few moments as a reward for him bringing it to you. If you have difficulty getting your dog to let go of the toy, try holding the toy firmly with one hand and placing a tasty tidbit in front of his nose

or waving another toy with the other. Just as you feel he is about to let go, give a signal such as "leave" so that you can eventually get him to let go on command.

◆ Practice these five stages often in short sessions, keeping them fun and enjoyable until your dog is happy to come back to you when he has a toy and begins to deliver the toy to you directly so that you can throw it again or play tug-of-war.

◆ Once you have an enthusiastic retrieve and your dog will happily bring back any toy you throw, teach him to sit and wait while you throw the toy. Ask him to retrieve the stationary toy when you give the signal to "fetch." Do this by taking hold of his collar and restraining him if he gets up too soon. Put him back into the sit and wait until you are ready before releasing him with an enthusiastic "fetch."

FETCH AND CARRY

Once your dog has mastered the basic retrieve, and will happily go and fetch any toy you point out to him, it is time to begin to teach him to fetch items other than his toys. When introducing a new item, make it into a retrieving game and keep it lighthearted. You want your dog to enjoy picking up the article, so keep it fun. Begin with soft items that are easy to carry, such as a slipper, and work up to harder objects that are

difficult to carry. Many dogs are put off by the feel of a brush's bristles or metal, so leave such objects until last. Progress gradually until your dog will go and fetch anything to which you point.

Once your dog will pick up just about anything you ask for, the next step is to teach him to carry things for you.

1 Ask your dog to fetch the article and, as he brings it to you, begin to walk away from him.

2 Keep encouraging him to come with you and turn around so that he is walking beside you.

3 After a few paces, make a big fuss over him and reward him well. If he drops the article at any time, quickly encourage him to fetch it again.

4 Progress slowly until he will walk beside you carrying anything you have asked him to fetch.

LEARNING NAMES OF OBJECTS

Once your dog is happy to pick up objects on command, you can begin to teach him the names for them. Try to begin with something familiar, such as his favorite toy. Combine his "fetch" command with the name of the article and repeat many times over several training sessions. Then do the same with a different article, such as a slipper.

You can then put the two articles

ABOVE: *When teaching your dog names of objects it's best to start off with familiar items, such as his toys, which he will find easy to identify and pick up.*

together and ask him to bring the one you ask for. If he brings the wrong one, do not scold him. Take it from him quietly and send him out again with the same command. When he brings the correct object, praise him enthusiastically and profusely. Continue in this way and he

THE CORRECT RESPONSE

Remember to praise profusely
whenever your dog shows the
correct response and ignore any
unwanted behavior.

will quickly learn the names of both
items. Once he has done so, you can add
more items to the list of names he knows,
using the same method.

FIND IT

It is useful to teach your dog to find items
that are not in view so that he can go
and fetch things from other rooms of the
house and so that he can play games that
involve finding hidden objects.

1 Begin by holding on to your dog's
collar and throwing a favorite toy so
that it lands out of sight, e.g., behind a
sofa or in long grass.

2 Wait for a few moments before you
release him to find it. Ask him to
"find" as he goes out to search for it.

3 After a few repetitions, walk him away from the place from which you threw the toy and turn him around a few times before releasing him to find it. Once he is happy to find an article that he has seen land, ask him to find one that you have placed in advance. Indicate the area you want him to search and place two or three large items in that area at first to insure he is successful.

Note: Practice this until he will go and search for items whenever you ask him to "find." Gradually progress until he will search the house or backyard for named items.

HELPING OUT

Once your dog has learned to carry items and fetch named items, he can be given useful things to do. For example, when you bring the shopping in, you can ask him to carry in his cans of dog food, or you can ask him to fetch your slippers or the newspaper or mail, or to pick up the pen you have dropped. Most dogs find it very rewarding to have a job to do and, if you remember to praise your dog well and sometimes reward him with tidbits or a game for helping you, you will both be benefiting from the experience.

PLAYING MESSENGER

This game involves teaching the dog to "go to" a named person in order to receive a reward. Messages can then be tucked into the dog's collar or you can teach him to carry a container that carries the message to that person. It can be fun to play this game with children and dogs.

1 Get your dog to sit beside you. Ask him to "go to" a named person who is sitting in the same room while getting up and moving toward that person.

2 As your dog approaches that person, they should produce a tidbit and lure him closer, feeding the tidbit as he gets there. Repeat this many times over several sessions until he runs over to that person as soon as you give the command.

3 Repeat stage 1 with the other person in the next room. Insure that the other person praises your dog enthusiastically and produces a tidbit when he arrives. Practice until you can send your dog to find that person anywhere in the house.

4 Repeat stages 1 and 2 using a different person.

TEACHING TRICKS

Tricks are easy to teach and, when performed, can be fun for both spectators and the dog. Never teach anything that is demeaning or undignified. Tricks should show others how clever your dog is and how nice it is to have a dog that is well trained.

Tricks that are easiest to teach are those that involve natural traits. For example, Terriers enjoy using their paws and are easy to teach tricks that involve pawing at something. Retrievers and other gun dogs like to use their mouths and are good at learning tricks that involve holding objects. Energetic, agile dogs enjoy tricks that involve running or jumping.

If you have mastered the basic exercises, and those in this chapter, teaching tricks should be quite easy. Choose simple tricks at first and work up gradually

BELOW: *Support the paw lightly rather than hold on, which may make him withdraw it.*

RIGHT: *Reward the desired behavior immediately with a tasty treat.*

to those that are more difficult. Always break up complicated tricks into stages and teach the last stage first. In this way, when you begin to teach an earlier stage, your dog will be moving towards a part of the trick that he knows and finds easy.

BE INVENTIVE

Like children, dogs get bored with doing things routinely. To get the best from your dog, be inventive about games, vary the tasks you set for him, and change the rewards every so often. If you do this, he will stay interested and willing to please, and you will have more fun too.

IDEAS FOR TRICKS

You can be as inventive as you like when teaching tricks, or you can choose one from this list.

◆ HI FIVE!
Give a paw.

◆ TELL ME WHICH ONE
Paw at the only pot containing food or a toy once they have been "shuffled."

◆ PRESS HERE FOR ACTION!
Press a pedal to get a treat.

BELOW: *"Tell me which one." By using his sensitive nose, this dog detects which pot the toy is under. He indicates this to his owner by touching it with a paw.*

WHEN THINGS GET DIFFICULT

If you are having difficulty teaching your dog part of the trick, write down what it is you want to achieve and see if it can be broken down into two smaller stages. This often helps to make it clearer. Try teaching a person to do the exercise without using words and ask them which part was most confusing . This does, of course, depend on how understanding your friends are and on the nature of the trick that you are trying to teach.

It is easy to get angry with your dog if he cannot understand what you want. End the session as soon as you begin to feel frustrated and think about what went wrong. Come back to it later when you are both fresh and try a different approach. Remember that teaching and performing tricks should be fun for both of you.

◆ **RUBBISH!**
Place an object in a box, e.g., put a candy wrapper in the trash can.

◆ **HOOPS**
Jump through a hoop.

◆ **DANCE WITH ME**
Weave in and out of your legs as you walk.

◆ **OVER!**
Jump a small jump.

◆ **FIND THE QUEEN**
Paw at the appropriate playing card.

◆ **SPEAK!**
Bark on command.

◆ **SSHH!**
Be quiet on command.

◆ **IT'S COLD IN HERE**
Shut the door.

◆ **ATCHOO!**
Pull a handkerchief out of a pocket and pass it to his owner.

ABOVE: *"Over!" Teach your dog to jump (but not until he is over 18 months old).*

COMPETITIONS

If you have a competitive nature or just want to show the world how clever and well trained your dog is, you may want to take part in a variety of competitions. They often include the following events.

AGILITY

Dogs learn to negotiate tunnels, hoops, high jumps, long jumps, high walks, and A-frames. This is then done around a set course at speed against the clock as in show jumping for horses. The handler runs around the course and controls the dog's direction with the dog off-lead. Dogs compete against others for the fastest time with fewest faults.

TRACKING TRIALS

Dogs learn to follow the path walked by a person several hours earlier. They

BELOW: *Agility courses often have a suspended tire for dogs to jump through.*

ABOVE: *Many dogs enjoy agility classes.*
This dog is negotiating the weaving poles.

also learn to search for dropped objects, and may have to negotiate various obstacles and surfaces. There are stakes of varying levels of proficiency and the sport is renowned for the friendliness of the competitors.

COMPETITION OBEDIENCE

Dogs learn to respond precisely to obedience commands, such as "heel," "sit," "stand," "down," and "stay." They learn how to retrieve a scented article from unscented ones and be sent away to a specified place. Precision is very important as handlers compete for points which are easily lost if positions are not exact.

FLYBALL

Dogs learn to run to a box by jumping a series of jumps, and then press a pedal on the box that delivers a ball which they retrieve to their handlers. Teams of dogs race against each other to see which are the fastest.

CHAPTER EIGHT

PROBLEM BEHAVIOR

Many behavioral problems will improve or even disappear altogether if the relationship between the owner and dog is improved, if all the essential needs of the dog are met, and if training is carried out correctly. There is not space here to go into all the behavioral problems and their solutions adequately but some advice has been given as a starting point.

TRY NOT TO RESORT TO PUNISHMENT

Bad behavior can be very frustrating for owners and there is a great temptation to resort to threats and violence to get a result. However, punishment rarely works

AGGRESSIVE DOGS

If your dog is aggressive, it is best to get expert help by contacting a good pet behavioral counselor. Either ask your veterinarian for a recommendation or contact the American Kennel Club at the address given (see page 126).

BELOW: *Chasing problems are common in the herding breeds. This behavior needs to be channeled into acceptable games with toys.*

and can harm the relationship between you, resulting in further problems. If your dog often engages in an unwanted behavior, then try to think through a possible solution that does not involve punishment. If you are unable to do so, seek further help from a good pet behavior counselor.

BAD MANNERS AND UNRULY BEHAVIOR

Teach good manners in the same way that you teach other exercises. Show your dog what you want him to do, give him praise and rewards for good behavior, and teach him a command for the required action. Since much unwanted behavior is self-rewarding, you will need to find a way to prevent it while you teach him how rewarding the appropriate behavior can be. To do this, use physical control to stop him from being rewarded by the unwanted behavior until he has learned good manners. Use gentle restraint, via a collar and lead, or remove whatever is causing the inappropriate behavior from temptation temporarily. You can then manipulate him into showing the correct behavior which can be rewarded. Over time, he will get into the habit of behaving as you want him to and will forget about behaving badly.

JUMPING UP
For example, if your dog jumps up when greeting you, he is doing so because he

BELOW: *Jumping up is an annoying habit that is easily controlled by using the right approach.*

wants to get closer to your face. Crouching down when greeting your dog enables him to get closer to you and reduces the need for him to jump up.

Alternatively, you can hold on to your dog's collar to prevent him from jumping up and tell him to "sit" instead (he must already know the meaning of "sit" if this is to work). Once he understands that as soon as he sits you crouch down and give him your undivided attention, he will be happy to comply with your request. Since jumping up is self-rewarding, ignoring the behavior will not work unless you can successfully turn your back on the dog and avoid touching, speaking, and looking at him until his four feet are on the ground.

If your dog jumps up or is badly behaved with visitors, look at how he greets you and behaves with you. If you get good manners from him when he is alone with you, he is much more likely to behave well when strangers are present.

If your dog is boisterous and out of control, teach him the exercises in Chapter 6 to give you some control. Look also at the amount of exercise he is getting since an underexercised dog is often boisterous and difficult to live with. It may also be a good idea to check your hierarchy rules (see Chapter 3), as difficult dogs may be too high in status and may need to be brought down to a lower level.

FEAR AND SHYNESS

Animals are often scared of things that are unfamiliar to them, especially if those things move and make loud noises. This trait helps to keep them safe in the wild and it has been handed down, via the genetic code, to our pet dogs today.

NOTHING TO BE ASHAMED OF

Behavioral problems are common and most dogs show some unwanted behavior on a regular basis. Dogs like to do things that owners find distasteful, such as eating feces, rolling in revolting substances, sniffing people's groins, or mounting the legs of visitors. If your dog has an embarrassing or annoying habit, it is unlikely that you will be alone. Behavioral problems are more common than you might think.

Consequently, dogs are often afraid of strangers, other dogs, children, things on wheels, noises, or a whole range of other things. This will be particularly true if your dog was not socialized well as a puppy (see page 21) and did not have enough different experiences when young to become familiarized with the world into which he would be taken out later. Dogs like this will spend a lot of their time being anxious and worried when taken into the outside world or when strangers come to visit.

Dogs may also become fearful of certain people, animals, or experiences because they have been frightened or hurt by them in the past. Consequently, dogs are often fearful of other dogs, strangers, or even owners who may have been overwhelming or aggressive. It only takes one or two unpleasant encounters for the fear to take root and, if it continues over a period of time, it can become generalized until the dog becomes afraid of all other dogs or people. Often, if the dog is sensitive and the thing causing the fear is something ordinary, such as a person or another dog, an owner will have no idea that their puppy has been scared by such experiences since they are unable to read the body language (see page 33). It is only later, as the puppy becomes more confident of itself, at about eight months old, that the problem is noticed. At this time, some aggression may be seen, even if it is only in the form

RIGHT: *Shy dogs need to be able to take things at their own pace so they can overcome their fears gradually.*

of barking and growling in an attempt to keep the thing that scares them away.

Whatever the reason for the fear, it is important not to force your dog to encounter something of which he is afraid. If you do, he is likely to learn to be aggressive either to keep the thing he is frightened of away or to prevent you from continuing to scare him.

◆   If your dog growls, barks, or snaps, it

is an indication that he is not happy with the situation. He cannot tell you in any other way. Rather than punish him, which is the natural reaction of most owners, try to appreciate that there is little else he can do to get himself out of what he sees as a potentially dangerous situation, and remove him from whatever it is that is upsetting him.

A good pack leader should protect his pack and if your dog sees you taking action in this way he is more likely to rely on you next time rather than dealing with the problem himself. It will be up to you to read his body language and anticipate what might scare him so that you can keep him out of trouble. Punishing him for growling may well stop him from doing so again, but you will not have made him less fearful. Instead, you will have removed his only means of communication that he is upset and he may well bite without warning when the fear becomes too great.

◆ If your dog is afraid of something, you will need to overcome his fear gradually by arranging for him to encounter whatever it is in a mild form first. This usually means putting distance between your dog and the thing he fears.

◆ Use games or tidbits to encourage him to have a happy time, and be lighthearted and jolly yourself, rather than being sympathetic or angry. When he can cope at a distance, gradually, over a number of sessions, move closer. Never go faster than

he can cope with and go back a stage if he shows signs of distress or anxiety. In this way, you can gradually desensitize him to what he used to be frightened of. Getting him to play with toys or concentrate on eating tasty tidbits can help to take his mind off the problem and change his attitude to a happy one instead.

◆ For example, if your dog is afraid of walking on the pavement next to noisy traffic and tries to bolt whenever a truck goes past, begin by taking him to an open space away from the road where he can see and hear noisy traffic in the distance. Relax and let him become accustomed to his surroundings. If he is still very wary at this distance, move farther away until he feels comfortable. Remain stationary, but give him as much freedom as possible by using either a long line or a flexi-lead. When he has settled, offer him games with toys and tasty tidbits. Have fun with him. Get him to the point where he is wagging his tail and is happy with life. Take a few paces toward the road, wait until he is relaxed, and play again. End the session while he is having fun and then return home without going near any major roads if possible.

Gradually, during many sessions over several weeks, you should begin to see an improvement in your dog's attitude to traffic. Eventually, your dog should be able to walk quite comfortably on the pavement next to the road. You may find that after using this method your dog turns and looks at you for a game with a toy or a tidbit when a particularly large, noisy truck goes past. This is normal and, by providing that game or tidbit, you will be reinforcing the message that there is nothing to worry about after all.

◆ Do not expect too much progress too soon. It takes a long time to overcome fears and replace them with a relaxed attitude. Imagine the thing you are most scared of (for example, spiders, snakes, speaking in public) and think how long it would take you to overcome your fear. Go slowly, letting your dog take things at a pace he can cope with, and you should, gradually, begin to see an improvement in his behavior.

PROBLEMS WHEN LEFT ALONE

Dogs can be destructive, noisy, or messy when left alone unless they are used to isolation. If your dog chews the furniture or doors, barks, howls, or messes when left alone, you will need to find out the cause before you can solve the problem.

There are many causes of separation problems but they fall into three distinct categories:
◆ Boredom/adolescent exploration
◆ Fear-based problems/insecurity
◆ Overattachment

BOREDOM
Bored dogs often chew or bark at the slightest disturbance just for something

to do. Adolescent dogs between the ages of six and twelve months often chew as they explore their environment. The secret to solving these problems is to tire them out, both physically and mentally, before you leave. A tired dog is usually asleep rather than engaging in unwanted behavior. In addition, leave tasty chews and interesting, safe objects to investigate when you are not there.

FEAR AND INSECURITY
Dogs who are frightened of something can often cope with the fear while you are present to protect them but become anxious when you leave. Dogs who are fearful often chew something that carries their owner's scent, try to dig a den into a mattress, chair, or under a table, and may defecate or urinate in fright as they begin to panic. These dogs need to be desensitized to whatever is frightening them. Leaving articles of clothing that smell of the owner in strategic places and making a denlike area in a dark, safe place can also be of temporary help.

OVERATTACHMENT
Dogs who are very attached to their owner or who are not accustomed to being left alone may make frantic attempts to get out of the house when left behind, damaging doors and frames in the process, or may bark and howl to attract their owner's attention. Such dogs need to be taught to

ABOVE: *A toy filled with tidbits provides excitement and interest for a dog with an active mind and can help to prevent problems caused by boredom when left alone.*

accept being left by leaving them for gradually increasing periods of time, beginning with a very short time initially.

CAR TRAVEL PROBLEMS

Most problems associated with car travel are those of excessive barking or frantic activity whenever the car is in motion. Again, the solution depends upon finding the cause. Owners will often attempt to

punish dogs that bark in the car. This rarely works because they are trying to treat the symptoms rather than looking at the underlying cause. Without removing the motivation for the behavior, the dog will continue to do what he wants to do and it will be very difficult for the owner to stop him. Instead, it is important to try to find out why he does what he does. In this way you can attempt to change the motivation behind his behavior, which is likely to be much more successful.

◆ Dogs can, for example, behave badly in the car because they are excited at the prospect of a walk. Dogs that bark for this reason are often those that only go into the car when they are going to be taken for an exciting walk. The association between being in the car and the walk is soon made and the dog begins barking with excitement in anticipation of getting out and having fun. Having a good game in the backyard to tire your dog out before putting him in the car, and taking him on journeys that do not end in a walk will help. In addition, it is wise to wait for at least five minutes at the end of any car journey or until he is calm and settled so that the car ride is associated with a boring wait when the car stops instead of wild activity. Take a magazine to read while you wait and, when you get out,

keep your dog on the lead for a while and do some quiet lead exercises with him before finally letting him loose.

◆ Dogs may also behave badly in the car because they are afraid of the movement (rather like us screaming when on a roller coaster). Such dogs will often be quite happy to sit in a stationary car but will start to become agitated as it begins to move. Some may drool and be sick, while others will be more active and may jump around and bark to relieve their anxiety.

BELOW: *Dogs that behave well in the car are more likely to be taken out more often.*

Dogs will often settle down on long journeys on straight roads, particularly highways, but will begin to get anxious again when the car begins to turn corners. These dogs will need to be desensitized gradually to being in the car and to its movement. In extreme cases, you may have to get them over their fear of getting into the car. This can be done by using toys and food to speed up the process. Get them feeling happy about sitting in a stationary car first. Then take them on very short journeys at first (possibly as short as a mile or two) and gradually build up to longer distances. Always end the journey with something enjoyable, such as a walk or dinner.

ABOVE: *Your dog will ride safer in a carrier. If left free, safety belt your dog to insure that he cannot interfere with your driving.*

◆ Dogs that enjoy chasing often become wildly excited in the car because they see things moving past them at speed. These dogs will often focus on something that is approaching, such as a tree or a person, and then spin around as it goes past. Since the dog is prevented from chasing the object, he often barks in frustration or may even resort to tearing chunks out of the upholstery. Dogs that do this need to be confined in such a way that prevents them from seeing out of the windows. This can be done by teaching them to lie on the floor by the passenger seat or by using a traveling carrier which is partially covered so they cannot see out.

◆ Dogs that bark at their owners while they are driving because they want attention often do this at home too. If your dog barks in the car while looking directly at you and also demands your attention at home, you will need to change his behavior in the house first before tackling the problem in the car.

DIFFICULT WITH OTHER DOGS

For solutions to problems of aggression toward other dogs, you would be well advised to find a good pet behavior counselor to help you. If, however, your dog only barks and gets excited when he sees another dog, it may be possible to focus his attention onto you instead. Most dogs bark and lunge forward because they

are fearful of other dogs and they have learned that behaving in this way keeps the other dog away from them. In addition, their owner often pulls them back so the distance between them and the dog they are scared of increases, which reduces the threat. Some dogs that show this behavior are fine when off the lead as they can run away or avoid other dogs. It is often only when they are on a leash with their owner and cannot get away that they have learned to behave badly.

With the advent of puppy socialization classes, there are an increasing number of

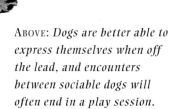

ABOVE: *Dogs are better able to express themselves when off the lead, and encounters between sociable dogs will often end in a play session.*

dogs that have learned to enjoy playing with other dogs and are desperate to get to them when they see them while out on a walk. Dogs that have been allowed to play many games with other dogs to the exclusion of games with their owners will often become very frustrated when their freedom is restricted by a lead. This frustration can cause aggressive behavior and it is often hard to tell the difference between this behavior and that caused by fear.

If you are experiencing problems of barking or excitement when your dog sees another dog (if it is severe, get professional help), you should be able to improve his

ABOVE: *Well-socialized dogs enjoy meeting others, but not all dogs will welcome their attentions.*

behavior by refocusing him onto you. Find an open space where dogs are playing in the distance. Allow him to settle and then invite him to play or to take tidbits from you. Use whatever motivates him most and praise him and reward him well for concentrating on you for a short time. If he would rather focus on the other dogs, wait until he has gotten bored with watching them and try again. (If he is taking a long time to stop looking at them, put more distance between you and them.)

If you have a friend who has a dog that your dog knows and is friendly with, you can begin practicing this procedure while their dog is walked around you in a wide circle.

Gradually, over time, and several sessions, move closer to where the dogs are playing until you can keep your dog focused on you even when the other dog is quite close. Eventually, you should be able to produce the toy or tidbits as a dog approaches and keep your dog's attention on you until after it has passed. Using toys or food in this way enables you to get him past other dogs in confined circumstances, such as on a pavement, and will help to prevent the problem from developing further. While you are working with this problem, you will need to avoid meeting dogs at close quarters or it will set back the progress and take longer to get a result.

CHASING

Dogs that chase things that they should not are usually either having fun or are trying to chase the things in question away. For dogs that enjoy chasing, particularly those from the herding breeds, their enjoyment needs to be channeled into acceptable games with toys. Dogs that are trying to chase things away because they are worried about them need to learn that those things are not dangerous.

EXCESSIVE BARKING

Barking is a normal behavior for dogs but can quickly become a problem if it happens often and for too long. Again, it is most important to find the cause of the problem.

◆ Dogs often bark to warn the rest of the pack of an intruder. This is acceptable behavior providing it is not sustained. Providing a distraction in the form of a game or tidbits will teach your dog to run to you at such times. It is a good way of taking his mind off whatever he is worried about and fixing it onto the reward, thereby quieting him.

◆ Your dog may have learned to bark when he wants attention. Saying anything to him, even if you are angry with him, will make him more likely to bark next time. The only way to stop it is to make a rule that you are not going to look at him, speak to him, or touch him, ever again, when he is barking. It can take some time to achieve, and it will get worse before it gets better, but it will work in the end.

◆ Teaching your dog to "speak" and "be quiet" on command will help him to understand what you mean when you ask him to stop barking.

OPPOSITE: *Teaching your dog to "speak" and "be quiet" on command will help him to understand what you mean when you ask him to stop barking.*

Useful information and addresses

Where to get further help

If your dog's problem is severe, seek further help. There are many "experts" in the world of dogs, but few people have the in-depth understanding that allows them to consider all aspects of your particular problem and come up with the right solution. Be very wary of anyone who claims to "know all about dogs" or who uses techniques that involve punishment or unpleasant methods. Try to find someone who keeps up to date with the current scientific literature on the subject, who is well read, and who knows the latest approach. They need to have been working with dogs for many years to gain the necessary experience and will use only effective, humane methods. A personal recommendation from someone who has tried out their methods or a referral from a veterinarian is often the best way to find the right person.

Useful addresses

American College of Veterinary Behaviorists
American Veterinary Medical Association
1931 North Meacham Road, Suite 100
Schaumburg, IL 60173-4360
Tel: 800-248-2862
http://www.avma.org

American Kennel Club
5580 Centerview Drive
Raleigh, NC 27606-3390

United Kennel Club
100 East Kilgore Road
Kalamazoo, MI 49001-5598

American Mixed Breed Obedience Registry (AMBOR)
205 1st Street S.W.
New Prague, MN 56071

INDEX